Justice and the Prosecution of Old Crimes

The LAW AND PUBLIC POLICY: PSYCHOLOGY AND THE SOCIAL SCIENCES series includes books in three domains:

Legal Studies—writings by legal scholars about issues of relevance to psychology and the other social sciences, or that employ social science information to advance the legal analysis;

Social Science Studies—writings by scientists from psychology and the other social sciences about issues of relevance to law and public policy; and

Forensic Studies—writings by psychologists and other mental health scientists and professionals about issues relevant to forensic mental health science and practice.

The series is guided by its editor, Bruce D. Sales, PhD, JD, University of Arizona; and coeditors, Stephen J. Ceci, PhD, Cornell University; Norman J. Finkel, PhD, Georgetown University; and Bruce J. Winick, JD, University of Miami.

***

The Right to Refuse Mental Health Treatment
    Bruce J. Winick
Violent Offenders: Appraising and Managing Risk
    Vernon L. Quinsey, Grant T. Harris, Marnie E. Rice, and Catherine A. Cormier
Recollection, Testimony, and Lying in Early Childhood
    Clara Stern, William Stern, and James T. Lamiell (translator)
Genetics and Criminality: The Potential Misuse of Scientific Information in Court
    Jeffrey R. Botkin, William M. McMahon, and Leslie Pickering Francis
The Hidden Prejudice: Mental Disability on Trial
    Michael L. Perlin
Adolescents, Sex, and the Law: Preparing Adolescents for Responsible Citizenship
    Roger J. R. Levesque
Legal Blame: How Jurors Think and Talk About Accidents
    Neal Feigenson
Justice and the Prosecution of Old Crimes: Balancing Legal, Psychological, and Moral Concerns
    Daniel W. Shuman and Alexander McCall Smith
Unequal Rights: Discrimination Against People With Mental Disabilities and the Americans With Disabilities Act
    Susan Stefan

Justice and the Prosecution of Old Crimes

Balancing Legal, Psychological, and Moral Concerns

Daniel W. Shuman
Alexander McCall Smith

AMERICAN PSYCHOLOGICAL ASSOCIATION

WASHINGTON, DC

Published by
American Psychological Association
750 First Street, NE
Washington, DC 20002

Copies may be ordered from
APA Order Department
P.O. Box 92984
Washington, DC 20090-2984

In the U.K., Europe, Africa, and the Middle East, copies may be ordered from
American Psychological Association
3 Henrietta Street
Covent Garden, London
WC2E 8LU England

Typeset in Times Roman by EPS Group Inc., Easton, MD

Printer: Data Reproductions Corporation, Auburn Hills, MI
Dust jacket designer: Ed Atkeson, Berg Design, Albany, NY
Technical/Production Editor: Amy J. Clarke

The opinions and statements published are the responsibility of the authors, and such opinions and statements do not necessarily represent the policies of the American Psychological Association.

Library of Congress Cataloging-in-Publication Data
Shuman, Daniel W.
    Justice and the prosecution of old crimes : balancing legal, psychological, and moral concerns / Daniel W. Shuman and Alexander McCall Smith.—1st ed.
        p. cm.—(The law and public policy)
    Includes bibliographical references and index.
    ISBN 1–55798–693–2 (hardcover : acid-free paper)
    1. Criminal law.   2. Prosecution.   3. Limitation of actions (Criminal law).   4. Victims of crimes—Legal status, laws, etc.
    5. Recovered memories.   I. McCall Smith, R. A.
    II. Title.   III. Series.
    K5015.S56   2000
    345—dc21   00-029277

British Library Cataloguing-in-Publication Data
A CIP record is available from the British Library.

Printed in the United States of America
First Edition

To Elizabeth McCall Smith and Emily Ruth Atlas

CONTENTS

INTRODUCTION

In recent years, a great deal of publicity has focused on the prosecution of crimes committed many years—or even decades—earlier. These cases have often attracted public interest because of the horrific nature of the crimes and the strong emotions that they engender. This has been evident in relation to efforts to address war crimes committed decades earlier, for example, in the case of recent French and Italian prosecutions for actions during World War II, and to come to terms with crimes committed by earlier governments against their own citizens in South Africa, Argentina, Chile, and Uruguay. One notable feature of the current wave of cases is that many of the allegations concern crimes of a sexual nature committed against children for which prosecution is only now, many years later, being sought. Many of those who have now come forward remained silent for years because of shame or confusion or because the perpetrator continued to hold sway over them. In some cases, the victims claim that their memory of what happened had been forgotten or lost until something triggered it much later in their adult life.

It should come as no surprise that each of these cases has generated considerable commentary. What is surprising, however, is that the press, courts, and scholars have treated the various categories of "old crimes" as unrelated. For example, although there are many excellent books and articles addressing the legal and psychological aspects of recovered-memory child sexual abuse cases, few authors have addressed the implications of these cases for war crimes prosecutions or have considered how both sorts of crimes would affect society's approach to statutes of limitations. We chose to write this book because we saw that the categories of cases raise numerous interrelated issues that are obscured if these prosecutions are viewed in isolation. It is our aim in this book, then, to examine how these cases and the issues they present are connected in our attempt to sort out which crimes should be left to the past and which should not.

How should people react to these crimes of the distant past? Should people encourage the criminals' prosecution in the timeless pursuit of justice, or should they draw a line at a certain point and say that what is past is past? This book is an examination of this troublesome and topical issue. Set against a background of actual cases, it provokes questions of responsibility and forgiveness. It also raises issues of memory and the responses of victims to these crimes. Finally, it asks at what point should the criminal law decline to revisit past wrongs.

In chapter 1, we look at the various sorts of crimes that may be prosecuted many years after their commission. We present a series of representative cases to raise the issues discussed in the course of the book, including two murders (the recovered-memory murder case of George Franklin in California and the murder of Steven Biko, a prominent political activist killed by South African security forces), a war crime (the attempt to deport and prosecute John Demjanjuk, claimed to be the operator of the gas chamber at the Treblinka death camp), and a sexual abuse case (a recent effort to prosecute child sexual abuse that is alleged to have occurred many years earlier).

What is the point of punishing old crimes? The decision whether to prosecute old crimes is made within the context of an existing criminal justice system and the justifications offered by that system to prosecute or decline to prosecute any crime. Thus, in chapter 2, we examine the various justifications for punishment, including retribution, deterrence, and rehabilitation, and ask how the passage of time between the crime and the institution of prosecution affects the state's interest in punishment.

We might expect that with the passage of time our willingness to forgive should increase, yet inappropriate forgiveness may be interpreted as condonation of wrong-doing. Chapter 3 addresses forgiveness of past wrongs. Although there is no merit in keeping alive dead issues, there are grounds for continuing to blame those who have perpetrated substantial wrongs. In this chapter, we examine the moral issues associated with forgiveness and mercy in a legal setting.

In chapter 4 we examine how the variations in the criminal law of different jurisdictions affect the right of the government to institute prosecution after the passage of a substantial time period. These statutes or prescriptions often play a critical gatekeeping role in the prosecution of old crimes. Although in the United States fixed periods of limitations exist for most crimes, excluding murder, that is not the case in other common law countries, such as Canada, England, and Australia. Are limitations simply an artificial constraint on the ability to prosecute old crimes? Or do they serve an important purpose in the criminal justice system that justifies non-prosecution?

Pardon and amnesty, which have particular application to the prosecution of old crimes, are standard features of all criminal justice systems. In addition to the special issues created by the use of pardon and amnesty to foster political transitions in South Africa, Argentina, Chile, and Uruguay, the passage of time itself makes criminals older and often seemingly less threatening. Chapter 5 addresses how the law should regard the passage of time on the exercise of the power to grant pardon and amnesty.

Chapter 6 addresses problems of proof in the prosecution of old crimes. Although any criminal prosecution may pose significant problems of proof, the prosecution of old crimes raises formidable challenges to human memory. Should the judicial system be willing to order the confinement or execution of a defendant on the basis of very old memories or in cases in which victims claim that their memories of the crime were once repressed but have now been recovered?

Criminal law does not claim to be a therapeutic tool for crime victims, yet the discretion that prosecutors enjoy to pursue old crimes often includes a consideration of the effect of prosecution on the victim. Chapter 7 addresses the impact of prosecution of old crimes on crime victims—an important albeit often unexamined issue. Does prosecution help with the recovery from traumatic events? Or does it merely reawaken painful memories? In this chapter, we examine the evidence for the effect of these proceedings on victims and how this varies in the case of delayed prosecution.

Finally, chapter 8 draws together the themes discussed in the other chapters to develop a principled approach for evaluating the prosecution of old crimes. As is the case throughout the book, our approach in chapter 8 is not to lecture or preach. You will not find a bright-line approach to when the prosecution of old crimes should be pursued and when it should be abandoned. Instead, our intention is to clarify the moral, legal, and psychological considerations that bear on these decisions.

ACKNOWLEDGMENTS

We are grateful to Bruce Feldthusen, Brandon Hamber, Amina Memon, Dan Stein, Thomas Wenzel, and Rachel Yehuda for their helpful insights and guidance in the creation of this book. We hope that they will find some of their wisdom captured here. Deans Paul Rogers, Harvey Wingo, and John Attanasio at the Southern Methodist University School of Law and the M. D. Anderson Research Fund generously supported our work.

Writing a book that draws on resources throughout the world cannot be done well without making great demands on library staff. Kurt Adamson, associate director of the Southern Methodist University Law Library, and his colleagues provided untiring assistance. To them we are greatly indebted.

We also thank our families—Elizabeth, Emily, and Lucy; Emily, Brooke, Lindsy, Julia, and Johanna—for their love and support during this project.

Justice and the Prosecution of Old Crimes

Chapter 1
ECHOES OF CRIMES PAST

Oh, this is a happy moment for us.[1]

With these words, Ellie Dahmer, the widow of Vernon Dahmer, a Black Mississippi storekeeper murdered in 1966, described her family's reaction to the conviction and life sentence of her husband's murderer, Samuel Bowers, a Ku Klux Klan official. There had been earlier murder trials, but in each case the jury had failed to agree on a verdict, and Bowers had been freed. Now, for Ellie Dahmer, justice was at last at hand, and she expressed relief and a sense of resolution commonly reported by victims of serious crime and their families when they believe that justice has been done. In her case, there had been a wait of more than 30 years; it was not until 1998 that her husband's murderer was finally brought to justice.

The politically charged events that took place in the South in the mid-1960s led to the commission of countless crimes of violence and intimidation.[2] Samuel Bowers, the man convicted of the murder of Vernon Dahmer, had already served a 6-year sentence for the federal crime of violating the civil rights of three young men who had engaged in voter registration campaigns to the displeasure of local segregationists. Despite of the existence of evidence linking a number of people to this killing, the state declined to bring murder charges, and it was left to federal prosecutors to seek a conviction for the only crime that was available to them: civil rights violations. These three murders remain unpunished—a matter that has not been forgotten by those involved in the events of those days. A typical view is that of a local Methodist minister who suffered directly for his involvement in the civil rights campaign. Although the society in which he lived has, in this respect at least, changed out of all recognition, he still says of the killings. "I want punishment. I want justice."[3] In this chapter, we introduce through a discussion of several notorious cases the special issues that the prosecution of old crimes pose. Beyond raising a series of questions that we develop at greater length in the chapters that follow, including problems of proof, limitations, the role of forgiveness and remembrance, and the therapeutic consequences of prosecution, we intend to impress the reader with the frequency with which we are faced with these issues and importance of these cases in shaping a just society.

Old Crimes Common and Uncommon

The fact that there are people who still wish to see 30-year-old crimes brought before the courts should not surprise us—at least in the specific context of these murders. The perpetrators of these crimes were stock villains: despicable bullies who sought to perpetuate oppression and fear through the use of bullets and firebombs. Their acts promote outrage, and the prospect of them answering for their crimes appeals to our sense of justice. After all, the victim's relatives are still alive and still feel the pain of what was done to them. Why should justice not run its course? Viewed as a simple matter of prosecuting a murder that so far has gone unpunished, it is difficult to see what objection there can be to bringing the matter to a conclusion by trying those thought to have committed the crime.

Murder seems to be a special case, however. Most legal systems and moral codes regard murder as the supreme wrong, and there is a strong view that it should be punished whenever it is discovered, even decades after the event. But what about other crimes—should they too be punished even decades after the event? This is a somewhat more difficult question, complicated by the existence in most legal systems of statutes of limitations, often inapplicable to murder, which set arbitrary limits to the time within which the state must bring most other criminal proceedings. The question is also complicated by the particularly emotive context in which the issue has arisen in recent years, namely, the sexual abuse of young people.

In a Dallas state court in 1998, a former Roman Catholic priest, Rudolph Kos, was sentenced to life imprisonment for his sexual assaults of four boys from 1981 to 1992.[4] The boys, all of whom were sons of parishioners, told the court a harrowing story of sexual abuse going back over a period of many years. Kos used both blandishments and threats to secure their compliance; now as young men, they described the effect of these incidents on their lives. In the victim impact statements—the opportunity for the crime victim to describe the harm that the crime caused—the trauma involved in the assaults was laid bare. In the words of one of the victims, Kos had stolen from him "the man I could have been." The prosecution, too, had strong—and emotive—words to describe what Kos had done, likening it to the "murder" of the boys' souls and inviting the jury to imprison the defendant for as long as possible.

The charges to which Kos answered were not the only ones that might have been brought against him. When he was attending an institution that the Catholic Church maintained for priests suspected of sexual wrongdoing, Kos was alleged to have confessed that he had been sexually involved with at least 20 boys. Charges were brought for another 2 of these but were dropped because the applicable Texas statutes of limitation require that criminal prosecution be instituted within 10 years of the commission of the offense or at least within 10 years of the date on which the victim of a sexual assault reaches his or her 18th birthday. Another of Kos's victims was dead, having committed suicide at the age of 21, allegedly as a result of his experience of years of abuse by the priest, making the state's proof of this abuse difficult, if not impossible.

The effect of the Kos prosecution on the Catholic Church is considerable. Not only did the church face the embarrassment of seeing one of its clergy exposed as an exploitative pedophile, but the financial consequences of the matter were to prove so serious as to prompt suggestions that the Diocese of Dallas would be driven into bankruptcy. In addition to the criminal charges brought against Kos, the church had to contend with the defense of an action for civil damages for its own failure to protect the altar boys from the priest's depredations. These civil claims have become a common feature of cases such as these; even if there is no prosecution—which may be for reasons of inadequate evidence or expiration of time limits—owing to the different interpretations of the civil statutes of limitation, often the victim may nonetheless file a civil claim against the perpetrator of the wrong. In many cases, the prospect of collecting a judgment may be unrealistic because the perpetrator may not have the funds to meet an award of damages. When the negligence is alleged against an organization like the Catholic Church, however, there may well be a point in litigation beyond that of emphasizing the wrong.

This proved to be so in the Kos case. In a civil action brought by 11 plaintiffs against the Catholic Diocese of Dallas and against Kos himself, the jury awarded the plaintiffs $119.6 million in damages. Church authorities, it was alleged, had been aware of the fact that Kos had pedophilic tendencies. His former wife (the marriage had been annulled) had warned them of his interest in boys, but her warnings had gone unheeded. The church, in ignoring the information brought before it—including a warning from another priest who had observed the comings and goings of boys to Kos's private rooms—failed to carry out a duty imposed on it under a child abuse reporting statute to inform local child protection officers of their suspicion that Kos had carried out acts of sexual abuse. This fact, together with other acts of negligence, resulted in a finding of civil liability against the church.

The Kos case is, regrettably, not unusual. Over the past decade, in a number of countries, the public has become accustomed to reading newspaper reports of the prosecution of priests and members of religious teaching orders for acts of sexual abuse dating back over decades. In Canada, there were several high-profile prose- cutions brought arising from the sexual abuse of boys in Catholic Church-run insti- tutions, and in Australia similar complaints were made against the staff of children's homes operated by the church.[5] One of the orders involved, the Irish Christian Broth- ers, which operated schools and children's homes in Canada and Australia as well as in Ireland itself, eventually issued an apology to those who had suffered abuse by its members.[6] What many of these cases have in common is the fact that the incidents are not fresh but go back some distance into the past.

Should these matters have been left to the past? In one view, this conduct involves an unnecessary raking over the coals of the past, and little point is served in going back over these wrongs committed many years ago. In the Kos case, there is a clear answer to such criticism. One very real concern is the risk that Kos was still a danger to children and had to be prevented from causing further harm. The complaints, then, were not entirely backward looking but could have major implications for the welfare of other young men who might find themselves coming under the priest's influence. There was also a widely expressed view that the damages awarded to the young men would have the effect of teaching the church the lesson that it had to take seriously the problem of pedophilic priests within its ranks. The philosophy of sweeping these problems under the carpet and treating pedophilic priests indulgently had to be rejected in the strongest possible terms, and financial penalties on the scale in question certainly may have that effect. Thus, arguments that legal actions of this sort, in cases of this kind, are an unjustified dwelling on the past seem frankly unconvincing.

It is not just priests and teachers who have been the subject of such complaints, however. The same newspapers that have reported the trial of defendants like Kos have carried numerous stories of charges brought against people who have carried out acts of sexual abuse that have involved perhaps an even greater degree of abuse of trust—the abuse of the trust that children place in their own families. Most sexual abuse of children takes place in the context of the home,[7] whether it is carried out by an older sibling, a parent, or some other person living under the same roof in a quasiparental role. The victims of these acts are often damaged in a profound way, as numerous psychological studies demonstrate, and may experience considerable psychosexual difficulties in adult life as a result.[8] Indeed, one of the particularly

distressing consequences of this situation is that abused children themselves often
become abusers in later life and may seek to explain their actions in terms of the
abuse that they themselves suffered.

In Canada, where there is no specific statute of limitations preventing the criminal prosecution of offenses of this nature, even decades after they were committed,
the courts have seen numerous allegations that these cases represent "stale offenses"
that should not be subject to punishment. The case of the Manitoba man known, for
legal reasons, as D. L. D. is a fairly typical example, involving the sexual abuse of
a child by her stepfather. The case came before the court early in 1991 and was
eventually disposed of by the Manitoba Court of Appeal in November 1992.[9] The
complainant was born in 1959. Although she alleged that she was first sexually
abused by her stepfather in 1963, when she was only 4 years old, the main incidents
of abuse were said to have taken place in 1967 and 1968, when she was 8 or 9 years
old. The complainant informed her mother about some of the incidents at an early
stage, but nothing was done about it. Then, in 1990, some 20 years after the events,
she informed the police, and criminal proceedings were instituted.

The striking thing about the prosecution is that it pertains to acts that occurred
so long ago. The defense was not slow to make much of this, arguing that the delay
in bringing the charges compromised the defendant's right to a fair trial protected
by the Canadian Charter of Rights and Freedoms. This lengthy delay, the defendant
argued, made it impossible to defend the charges leveled against him. In this case,
the argument was dismissed, and the court recognized that in the special circumstances of child sexual abuse, there are often good reasons why a complaint cannot
be made until many years after the event. Other cases of delayed prosecution have
met with similar results despite the concern expressed in some courts as to the
wisdom of proceeding with prosecution in these circumstances.[10]

A Canadian prosecution that attracted a great deal of attention was that of the
former premier of Nova Scotia, Gerald Regan. In 1998, Regan was acquitted of eight
charges of sexual assault against women. Some of these charges dated back to 1956;
others related to the late 1960s. The case cost taxpayers millions of dollars, and the
entire process of investigation and trial lasted over 5 years. Commenting at the end
of the trial on the difficulties in mounting a defense to matters dating back so far,
Regan's attorney noted that

> I would hope this trial may be a watershed case for a public debate over whether it
> is time in Canada to have a statute of limitations on these old charges. It is no longer
> acceptable to put somebody through a charge that is forty-two years old, except for
> a charge of murder.[11]

These cases are examples of allegations that have resulted in prosecution despite
the lapse of time, and in some of which, the convictions that the victims (or their
families) have demanded have been secured. Not all the wrongs of the past are
redressed, however, particularly if they are committed by the agents of the state.
Even if there were a State Attorney General in Mississippi who was prepared to
bring charges for a murder committed 30 years ago, there have been many prosecutors and justice officials elsewhere who have been either opposed to bringing
charges or politically prevented from doing so.[12] One principled argument supporting
this action is that there are circumstances in which the criminal law should ignore
the past and refrain from bringing charges. This view often comes into its own at

moments of political transition, when there has been a break with the political past or a civil war—or its undeclared equivalent—has been brought to an end. There are strong pragmatic arguments in favor of such a policy, but there are also numerous voices raised against it, many of which speak with passion.

Policies of nonprosecution of crimes committed in a previous political era have been followed, most notably, in Central America and South Africa.[13] The crimes in question are all too common to totalitarian regimes: torture, disappearance, rape, and summary execution, usually at the hands of security services and with the connivance of politicians. Typically, the authorities deny any knowledge of the crimes and frustrate attempts at investigation or, if they accept responsibility, they justify their conduct by reference to reasons of state. In South Africa's case, many of the crimes committed in the era of apartheid—itself declared an international crime by a United Nations resolution but never prosecuted—were justified by the authorities as being part of the struggle against the "total onslaught" of communism on the country. In fact, the crimes committed were tawdry acts of terror, in many cases carried out against political opponents who were unable to find any legitimate means of expressing their political rejection of the system.[14]

The hearings of the South African Truth and Reconciliation Commission brought to public attention many politically motivated acts of violence or homicide that had previously escaped detection or that had never been solved. One of the best known of these is the death in police custody of Steve Biko, a prominent political activist who died in a police cell in 1977.[15] Biko's death was never satisfactorily explained by the authorities at the time. An inquest that ruled that he had died as a result of blows received from unknown people failed to satisfy his family and the public, and it was widely—and correctly, as it turned out—assumed that he had died as a result of police brutality during an interrogation. Biko came to be regarded as a martyr of the South African struggle against racial oppression, and it is not surprising that many were keen to see the uncertainties surrounding his death resolved. As in the Mississippi killings, there were many who simply wanted to know exactly what had happened in the police cells and, in particular, who had administered the fatal blows.

In normal circumstances, this desire to know the truth might be answered by a trial, with a defendant arraigned in open court and called to account for what he had done. In the Biko case, however, we see a different facet of the resolution of old crimes with the invocation of a radically different approach to the wrongs of the past—an approach based not so much on accusation and punishment but on the ascertaining of the truth with a view to reconciliation and healing.

After the transition from apartheid, the South African Parliament was faced with two courses of action. Since 1948, when the segregationist National Party had taken power, a massive apparatus of oppression had been erected. This had not only resulted in the physical dispossession of the land and houses of many who found themselves on the wrong side of racially defined land boundaries but also ruthlessly crushed any serious political opposition. Although the system worked within a legal framework, with overt respect for the rule of law, the law itself was profoundly unjust. Inevitably, those charged with the policing of the system engaged in acts of brutality, including torture. There were many who, like Biko, met their end at the hands of the police or army. South Africa, of course, was not alone on the African continent in resorting to state violence on a substantial scale.[16] Other regimes in independent Africa behaved with an equal lack of respect for human rights. Idi

Amin's Uganda was one of the best known examples of this lack of respect for human rights; however, in the South African case, the wrongs struck many as being particularly offensive because of their calculated, cold nature and, at least for those abroad, because they were a vivid and awkward reminder of past injustices committed by White people against Black people. Apartheid had its victims, and they were now faced with a situation where power had been transferred from oppressor to oppressed.

It would have been theoretically possible for the new government to engage in a wholesale process of investigating and prosecuting the crimes of the apartheid era. This would have resulted in numerous trials and the punishment of many of those who perpetrated acts that were, after all, crimes even according to the law of the *ancien régime*. Yet such a course of action would likely have had serious political and economic consequences. It was not in the interests of the new state to start its existence in an atmosphere of division. The majority of those who assumed power were painfully aware of the wounds that the old ideology had caused and the bitterness it had generated. The rhetoric of the African National Congress, the dominant party in the new government, had always been that of inclusiveness, and to take a measure that could be calculated to alienate a substantial minority would hardly help to bring communities together. There were also strong economic arguments against alienating the White minority, which still controlled the economy and still constituted the largest part of the highly skilled and professional workforce. Finally—and it is difficult to assess the role of this single factor—there was the personality of a new president, Nelson Mandela, whose conciliatory attitude had stunned the international community into admiration. It is significant that Mandela himself sought out Percy Yutar, the man who had led the prosecution team at the Rivonia treason trials, which had resulted in Mandela's conviction for sabotage and imprisonment for nearly 4 decades, and who had, by all accounts, been a particularly zealous prosecutor. At his meeting with Yutar, Mandela avoided any recrimination and treated his former adversary with manifest courtesy and respect.

The attitude of the new state to the wrongs of its past is demonstrated in the final clause of the new South African Constitution:

> This Constitution provides a historic bridge between the past of a deeply divided society characterized by strife, conflict, untold suffering and injustice, and a future rounded on the recognition of human rights, democracy and peaceful coexistence and development opportunities for all South Africans, irrespective of color, race, class, belief or sex.
>
> The pursuit of national unity, the well-being of all South African citizens and peace require reconciliation between the people of South Africa and the reconstruction of society.
>
> The adoption of this Constitution lays the secure foundation for the people of South Africa to transcend the divisions and strife of the past, which generated gross violations of human rights, the transgression of humanitarian principles in violent conflicts and a legacy of hatred, fear, guilt and revenge.
>
> These can now be addressed on the basis that there is a need for understanding but not for vengeance, a need for reparation but not retaliation, a need for ubuntu [humanity] but not for victimization.[17]

These goals were to be achieved by an amnesty for politically motivated crimes committed before the transition. More importantly, however, amnesty was conditional on public disclosure of what had been done. As the new Minister of Justice, Dullah Omar, explained,

> I could have gone to Parliament and produced an amnesty law—but this would have been to ignore the victims of violence entirely. We recognized that we could not forgive perpetrators unless we attempt also to restore the honor and dignity of the victims and give effect to reparation. The President believes—and many of us support him in this belief—that the truth concerning human rights violations in our country cannot be suppressed or simply forgotten. They ought to be investigated, recorded and made known. I wish to stress that the objective of the exercise is not to conduct a witch hunt or to drag violators of human rights before court to face charges. However, it must be stressed that a commission is a necessary exercise to enable South Africans to come to terms with their past on a morally accepted basis and to advance the cause of reconciliation. I invite you to join in the search for truth without which there can be no genuine reconciliation.[18]

The Truth and Reconciliation Commission not only concerned itself with establishing the broad pattern of what had happened under apartheid but also gave an opportunity to individual victims to find out the truth of events in which they had been involved and to relate, in public, what they had suffered.[19] This was rather different from giving evidence at a trial; but just as at a trial, it involved reading the details of personal suffering into a public record—a public act with a therapeutic goal, to which we return later. The hearing into the death of Steve Biko was, naturally, one of the more prominent of such occasions, but the commission heard numerous accounts from lesser known victims and perpetrators.

The prospect of amnesty flushed out one of the police interrogators who had participated in the assault on Biko. It is significant, though, that his appeal for amnesty was opposed by the Biko family, who had challenged the constitutionality of the amnesty law itself. Their argument before the Constitutional Court was that this legislation was in conflict with the provision of the Constitution that provided that every person should have the right to have justiciable disputes settled by a court of law or other appropriate forum. There were technical reasons why this appeal should fail—the wording of the Constitution clearly authorized amnesty as an exception to the general principle of court resolution of disputes; but there were also strong policy reasons why the court should protect the concept of nonpunishment. In this respect, the judgment of Justice Mahommed is instructive. He understood "perfectly why the applicants would want to insist that those wrongdoers who abused their authority and wrongfully murdered, maimed or tortured very much loved members of their families . . . should vigorously be prosecuted and effectively be punished for their callous and inhuman conduct in violation of the criminal law."[20]

The judgment goes on to say that

> every decent human being must feel grave discomfort in living with a consequence which might allow the perpetrators of evil acts to walk the streets of this land with impunity, protected in their freedom by an amnesty immune from constitutional attack, but the circumstances in support of this course require carefully to be appreciated. . . . Much of what transpired in this shameful period is shrouded in secrecy and not easily capable of objective demonstration and proof. . . . Secrecy and authoritarianism have concealed the truth in little crevices of obscurity in our history. Records are not easily accessible, witnesses are often unknown, dead, unavailable or unwilling. All that often effectively remains is the truth of wounded memories of loved ones sharing

instinctive suspicions, deep and traumatizing to the survivors but otherwise incapable of translating themselves into objective and corroborative evidence which could survive the rigors of the law. The Act seeks to address this massive problem by encouraging these survivors and the dependants of the tortured and the wounded, the maimed and the dead to unburden their grief publicly, to receive the collective recognition of a new nation that they were wronged, and crucially, to help them to discover what did in truth happen to their loved ones, where and under what circumstances it did happen, and who was responsible. That truth, which the victims of repression seek so desperately to know is, in the circumstances, much more likely to be forthcoming if those responsible for such monstrous misdeeds are encouraged to disclose the whole truth with the incentive that they will not receive the punishment which they undoubtedly deserve if they do. Without that incentive there is nothing to encourage such persons to make the disclosures and to reveal the truth which persons in the positions of the applicants so desperately desire.[21]

The judge did not find the alternatives to this policy of encouraging disclosure to be at all attractive. He suggested that if the right to prosecute were to be preserved, this would leave the matter unresolved, possibly for an indefinite period. The families of those who had suffered would remain ignorant of what had happened, simply because it may never be possible to gather enough evidence to bring the culprits to trial. This, he said, would prolong and possibly increase their trauma. The perpetrators, too, would be unable to make a fresh start; they might well carry with them a burden of guilt that would cripple them as useful citizens of the new state.

This humane and perspicacious judgment neatly encapsulates the central dilemma in the Biko case and in so many others like it. The South African approach contrasts sharply with the approach that fuels the demands for justice in Mississippi or in the sexual abuse cases of the Kos variety. What should we do about crimes of the past? Should a line of closure be drawn after the passage of a certain length of time, or should we persist in the investigation and prosecution of wrongs whenever they were committed? These wrongs may be very old indeed and, in fact, may only be remembered by those who are very old. But many believe that the age of a wrong is no bar to keeping it alive. In its 1997–1998 session, for example, the Belgian Senate officially recognized the fact that the Ottoman Empire had carried out a program of genocide against the Armenians in 1915, calling on the Turkish government to acknowledge the crime.[22] In the same year, the British government officially announced that it would not give a posthumous pardon to those soldiers who were executed for cowardice in the World War I who were likely to have been suffering from what is now recognized as posttraumatic stress disorder.[23] This angered a substantial lobby who had been calling for the measure. Some wrongs clearly continue to resonate for a very long time. Can we identify some means of distinguishing between those wrongs that should be consigned to the past and those that should continue to require a formal legal response?

Prosecuting Old Crimes: Can We Be Sure?

An initial objection to the prosecution of old crimes is the difficulty of proof. It is a fundamental requirement of a criminal justice system that there should be a conviction only if it is convincingly established that the accused committed the offense charged. In some cases, evidence of guilt may be beyond question; in others, it may be less overwhelming but may still be sufficient to satisfy the common-law standard of proof beyond a reasonable doubt. The meaning of the phrase beyond a reasonable doubt is, of course, a matter of debate. Clearly, however, it means more than a belief that the accused is more likely than not guilty—the standard of proof in a civil action. It requires a high degree of certainty that the accused did what he or she is said to have done.

Proving guilt beyond a reasonable doubt is difficult enough in the run-of-the-mill criminal case. Many prosecutors find it difficult to explain to complainants or their families that criminal proceedings may not be pursued because of inadequate evidence. Yet the decision not to proceed to a trial is a necessary option for prosecutors because of the economic and political costs of bringing a prosecution that will simply not result in a conviction. If this is true of recent crimes, then how much more difficult is the prosecution of crimes that were perpetrated many years before?

The law asks that a witness provide an accurate account of past events. An accurate accounting permits the court or jury to convict or acquit based on what actually happened. Human memory, however, is personal and subjective.[24] People do not record images like a camera or a computer to recall them accurately whenever they choose to do so. Thus, our memories of both recent and distant events are often not as reliable as we may assume. This may be because of failures to encode an impression in the first place or because the processes of retrieval are faulty. Some memories persist over the years; others are effectively lost or become less clear and, therefore, less reliable. The process of aging itself may have an effect on a person's ability to remember events, as may intervening illness. For all these reasons, a person giving an account of what happened a decade ago may not be able to speak to the event as reliably as one recounting an event that occurred a few months before.

If there must be some doubt about the reliability of memories of the distant past, even greater controversy surrounds memories that are said to have been repressed for years and that now surface and result in a criminal accusation. The murder prosecution of George Franklin is an example of a case in which such memories were relied on to bring charges for a murder that had gone unsolved for 20 years. The 8-year-old victim in this case, Susan Nason, was sexually assaulted and brutally murdered; her body was discovered on a beach outside of San Francisco in 1969.[25] The investigation of this rape and murder led to no arrests or prosecution until 20 years later. Then Nason's best friend, Bonnie Franklin-Lipsker, claimed that precipitated by looking at her own daughter, she recalled that she had witnessed her father's (George Franklin's) rape and murder of Nason, which she had repressed since the time of the killing. Franklin-Lipsker's husband persuaded her to inform the police about her memories of the rape and murder, and her father, who was still alive at the time, was in due course prosecuted and convicted, in large part on the basis of his daughter's recovered memories.

This case demonstrates the extraordinary problems of proof in cases of old crimes. Although there may be no principled reason to fail to prosecute such a case 20 years later, there may be practical reasons for failing to do so. In this case, the prosecution's case relied on a controversial psychological claim that it is possible to repress once-viable memories of an event and to recover these memories intact many years later. Sharp disagreement exists whether there is any basis in research on memory to think that this can occur or whether these memories are likely to result from suggestive questioning or other contaminating influences.[26] In addition to memory issues that raise problems of proof in the prosecution of old crimes, there are also problems of loss of proof or destruction of evidence. A federal district court ultimately reversed Franklin's conviction on the basis of the prosecution's failure to turn over potentially exculpatory evidence to the defense, as it was constitutionally required to do. Although the state could, as a matter of law, have retried the defendant, it concluded that it could not then marshal the evidence to do so. In principle, we ought to recognize no bar to prosecution for serious offenses like rape and murder from the mere passage of time; however, the passage of time presents serious and often fatal practical problems with successful prosecution.

A more basic objection may arise over the question of the identity of the defendant. The linking of a defendant with a crime depends on satisfactory identification, and this, as is the case with the recall of events, may be compromised by the passage of time. A controversial example of identification problems is that of the deportation from the United States and the subsequent prosecution of John Demjanjuk.[27] According to a number of survivors of the Nazi concentration camp at Treblinka, Demjanjuk was the man known to them at the time as "Ivan the Terrible," a sadistic camp official who participated in countless murders.[28] Demjanjuk's defense was simple: He was not the man in question, and the eventual conclusion of the Supreme Court of Israel was that there was indeed sufficient doubt in his favor to justify setting aside his conviction.

Forgiving and Forgetting

Even if there is reliable evidence that the defendant committed the crime charged, principled objections to the prosecution of old crimes may remain founded on the notion that it is simply vindictive to bring charges for an offense that took place so many years before. Alternatively, the argument may be that seeking punishment in these circumstances demonstrates an unforgiving attitude. In this view, there are strong reasons to forgive the wrongs of the past: Keeping them alive merely perpetuates ill feeling and prevents social healing. Forgiveness is widely seen as a balm that enables one to resolve the feelings of distress that one has experienced as a result of another's wrongful acts.

The idea of forgiveness is increasingly being advocated by therapists, both lay and professional.[29] Forgiveness is nothing new in religious debate; indeed, the notion that one should forgive others forms a central tenet of much religious thinking. It is only comparatively recently, however, that mental health professionals have begun to stress the role that forgiveness plays in a person's recovery from trauma. The recommendation of forgiveness comes, then, not merely as a matter of moral duty but as a matter of personal restoration. A start has now been made in studying empirically the positive effects of forgiveness on psychological health. In one pilot study, Freedman and Enright examined the effect of forgiveness in a group of 12 incest survivors.[30] The participants were divided into two groups: (a) those in whom a program of encouraging and facilitating forgiveness would be initiated and (b) a control group in which it would not. Those who forgave their abusive male relative showed a significant reduction in anxiety levels and depression. Those who did not start the process of forgiveness continued to harbor a high level of negative emotions and depression. Remarkably, once the control group was put on the forgiveness program, they too began to show improvements similar to the original forgiving group.

Needing to Remember: Rehearsing the Past

The idea that one should be reluctant to punish past wrongs is strongly rejected by many contemporary human rights activists, particularly by those involved in the monitoring of human rights violations of totalitarian regimes in Central and South America.[31] If we fail to identify and punish the wrongs of the past, they have argued, those who oppress others will be able to do so with impunity. This impunity, they have argued, is not only practically dangerous, in that it gives a green light to those who resort to torture and murder, but it also obliterates the historical record. This historical record, they have argued, is precisely what the relatives of those who have been killed so desperately want to establish. Similarly, the authorities may wish to use trials for "show purposes" to create or reinforce a public memory. The rights of victims may not be the main concern; the aim may be to present a vivid public interpretation of a traumatic event in such a way that its collective meaning becomes fixed.[32]

There are numerous recent examples of calls to use judicial and similar processes to throw light on past political oppression. We have already seen how this was one of the rationales of the Truth and Reconciliation Commission in South Africa; the same phenomenon has occurred in countries such as Guatemala and Haiti, where decades of authoritarian government resulted in widespread abuses of fundamental human rights. Guatemala provides a particularly instructive—and bleak—instance of the tension between a policy of amnesty and a policy of pursuing the truth about past atrocities. For those who oppose amnesty, the Guatemalan example demonstrates the need for formal proceedings to clarify the historical record and to prevent future abuses. Since the late 1970s, over 100,000 people are assumed to have been killed in the course of the counterinsurgency campaign waged by the Guatemalan government. Most of these victims were not involved in antigovernment activities but were innocent civilians, often indigenous people. The massacres were carried out by the military and civil defense forces, and the victims were frequently buried in anonymous mass graves, many of which have yet to be excavated. The dispute between the government and the armed opposition was settled in 1996; in that same year, the Congress passed a Law of National Reconciliation, which granted an amnesty for grave crimes committed—for political motives—during the conflict.

Although the amnesty law was part of a peace settlement that embodied some important concerns of those who had taken up arms against the government, there has been organized resistance to it, including a constitutional challenge by an organization known as the Alliance Against Impunity.[33] Significantly, there has also been opposition to impunity on the part of Amnesty International, which has closely monitored human rights abuses in Guatemala. In Amnesty International's view, there may be a role for pardon, but this should only be given after prosecution in open court and, if appropriate, conviction, sentencing, and provision of compensation to the victim.[34] Amnesty International has charted significant and continued human rights abuses, including numerous killings by agents of the state, since the peace accord, strengthening the claim that a failure to investigate and punish past wrongs merely perpetuates a culture of impunity in which wrongs will continue to be perpetrated.

Opponents of amnesties and unearned forgiveness in Guatemala are concerned that those whose relatives have "been disappeared" (a sinister term in the Central and South American context) will be denied an important right if their quest for accountability is not met. The strength of this has been recognized by the United Nations in the *Principles* adopted by the Subcommission on the Prevention of Discrimination and Protection of Minorities.[35] These principles state that not only do people have a right to know about the background of systematic violations of human rights, but there is also a "duty to remember" on the part of the state. At a personal level, the families of victims have what is described as an "imprescriptible right" to know the truth about the fate of the victim.

The determination with which human rights activists press the case against impunity must give any advocate of forgiveness cause to reflect. The appeal of forgiveness is strong, and its rhetoric frequently moving; yet the cause of forgiveness in the Guatemalan case is muted, although presumably it has its supporters other than those who stand to benefit from the nonprosecution of their crimes. What we are confronted with is two radically differing visions of the best course of action in the aftermath of substantial and prolonged wrongs: a course of forgiveness, such as that promoted in South Africa, and a course of formal investigation and prosecution, such as that promoted by the anti-impunity movement. Note that there is no serious case made for deliberate forgetting; nobody advocates amnesia except those who have the most to hide.

Forgetting the past has implications beyond the danger of denying those who have suffered a sense of the historical place of their suffering. Criminal proceedings play an important role in deterring wrongful conduct; there may be reasons for forgiveness and for refraining from exacting punishment, but the gains of this approach have to be set against the weakening of the deterrent effect of the law. It is this problem that motivates many of those who call for the prosecution of human rights offenders, whatever the political circumstances and whatever time has passed since the commission of the crime. If the message is not conveyed that war crimes will be punished wherever or whenever the perpetrator is apprehended, people are encouraged to think that they can act with impunity and never face justice.

Justice and Therapy: The Role of Law in Healing the Victim

The view that law should adopt therapeutic goals is a relative newcomer to criminal jurisprudence.[36] For example, the criminal law has not, traditionally, treated the interest of the victim as a central concern but has focused instead on issues of individual guilt and formal disposal. The conduct of the defendant—and the harm caused to the victims—may be taken into account in sentencing, but beyond that a conventional criminal trial does not necessarily concern the question of whether the prosecution has benefited the victim. The fact that a complaint has been made, of course, is an indication that the victim wishes criminal proceedings to be instituted, and the same may be said of the fact that the victim is prepared to give evidence. Victims' expectations about the consequences of a prosecution, however, may not reflect what crime victims who have prosecuted their wrongdoers experience in their involvement with the criminal justice system and its impact on their recovery. Crime victims who thought punishment would bring closure have not invariably found this to be so.[37] It is possible that the standard assumptions about victims' emotional needs to see wrongdoers punished are mistaken and that prosecution may be irrelevant to recovery or may hinder rather than assist recovery.

There is good reason to consider these issues carefully in the prosecution of old crimes. Presently, only notorious crimes that are not prosecuted in a timely manner are likely to be subject to delayed prosecution; most "ordinary" crimes that are not prosecuted in a timely manner are never prosecuted and, of course, in many instances, there are decisions not to prosecute even notorious old crimes. Prosecutors may exercise their discretion not to prosecute notorious old crimes when they conclude that it would not be in the public interest to do so. If prosecution is an essential step in crime-victim recovery, however, society may have a special obligation to crime victims to consider the prosecution of crimes whenever they are discovered. This would seem to have relevance to the campaigns against impunity in Central and South America and in Africa, which have challenged the failure to prosecute crimes of a past regime. In particular, the importance of prosecution in crime victims' recovery raises serious questions about the likely impact of the South African Truth and Reconciliation Commission on victims of crimes of the apartheid era, reinforced by preliminary observations of therapists working with these victims, that amnesty has not helped the recovery of these victims.

Alternatively, what if prosecution is not an essential element in crime victims' recovery or is in some instances harmful to those victims forced to confront disturbing events they have consigned to the past? Does society owe crime victims a role in deciding whether there will be a prosecution? What of the effects of testifying on Holocaust survivors asked to identify John Demjanjuk as the Treblinka gas chamber operator; was the opportunity for justice therapeutic for them, or did it require them to confront memories that they sought to relegate to the past? What of the state's decision to prosecute the man alleged to have murdered Susan Nason 20 years earlier; what was the likely effect on the victim's surviving family of the state's decision to prosecute that horrible crime so long after its occurrence, relying on evidence that many researchers regarded as unreliable? Given these possible benefits and risks, what role should the victims or their families have played in the decision to prosecute the case 20 years after the crime? Whether we acknowledge it by according victims a role in the decision to prosecute old crimes and whether we study the issue formally, the prosecution of old crimes presents significant potential benefits and significant potential risks for crime victims and their families.

It is easy to support the notion that in an ideal world, the commission of a crime should inevitably lead to prosecution. This view accords with our sense of justice in that we expect the consistent and impartial application of the criminal law. Yet clearly the issue is much more complicated than that, and in the case of some old crimes, the prosecution may help neither the victim nor society. The difficulty is in identifying these cases and in distinguishing them from those cases in which nonprosecution would be unjust and unhelpful. We must also bear in mind that the prosecution implies the possibility of punishment. For those who espouse forgiveness, the punishment of crimes of the distant past may seem vindictive and unproductive. It is this concern to which we now turn.

Endnotes

1. Larry Copeland, "After 5 trials, ex-Klansman convicted in Miss." *USA Today*, Aug. 24, 1998, at 3A.
2. See, e.g., Jack Bass, *Taming the storm: The life and times of Judge Frank M. Johnson and the South's fight over civil rights* (New York: Doubleday, 1993); William Maxwell McCord, *Mississippi: The long hot summer* (New York: Norton, 1965).
3. D. Oshinsky, "Should the Mississippi Files have been reopened?" *The New York Times*, Aug. 30, 1998, Sec. 6, at 30.
4. "Kos abuse victim says he can 'never forgive,' " *The Fort Worth Star–Telegram*, Apr. 2, 1998, Thursday, *Arlington AM Edition News*, at 17.
5. Neil Leslie, "Christian brothers face wave of abuse claims: Founder's descendant to sue," *The Mirror*, Oct. 25, 1999.
6. Michael Foley, "Brothers apologize after 'long hard' think," *The Irish Times*, Mar. 30, 1998, at 3.
7. Some studies suggest that sexual abuse outside the home is actually exceptional. *See* W. N. Friedrich, R. L. Beilke, and A. L. Urguiza, "Behavior problems in young sexually abused boys," *Journal of Interpersonal Violence*, 3 (1988):21–28.
8. Bill Watkins and Arnon Bentovim, "Male children and adolescents as victims." In *Male victims of sexual assault*, Gilian C. Mezey and Michael B. King, Ed. (Oxford, England: Oxford University Press, 1992) at 27–66.
9. 77 Canadian Criminal Cases 3d 426.
10. See, for example, *W. K. L. v. R.*, 64 CCC 3d 321, where the misgivings of the trial judge are examined by the Supreme Court of Canada.
11. Kelly Toughill, "Not guilty," *Toronto Star*, Dec. 19, 1998.
12. Gregory Padgett, "Comment. Racially motivated violence and intimidation: Inadequate state law enforcement and federal civil rights remedies," *Journal Criminal Law and Criminology* 75 (1984):103–138.
13. A. James McAdams, Ed., *Transitional justice and the rule of law in new democracies* (Notre Dame, IN: University of Notre Dame Press, 1997).
14. Tracy Kuperus, *State, civil society, and apartheid in South Africa: An examination of Dutch-Reformed Church–state relations* (New York: St Martin's Press, 1999).
15. David Yutar and Beauregard Tromp, "South Africa; The Biko, Benzien amnesty poser," 1999 *Africa News Service, Inc.*, Feb. 22, 1999.
16. *Azanian Peoples Organization, Biko and others v. the President of the Republic of South Africa and others*, 1996 Case CCT 17/96 (CC), *South African Constitutional Law Reports*, LEXIS 20.
17. Constitution of the Republic of South Africa, 1993, Act No. 200 of 1993.
18. Statement by Dullah Omar on the creation of the Truth and Reconciliation Commission under the Promotion of National Unity and Reconciliation Act, No. 34 of 1995.
19. There is now an extensive literature on the South African Truth and Reconciliation Commission. A particularly useful accounting is provided by: Martha Minow, *Between vengeance and forgiveness* (Boston: Beacon Press, 1998).
20. *South Africa Constitutional Law Review*, LEXIS 20, 36 (1996).
21. *Azanian Peoples Organization, Biko and others v. the President of the Republic of South Africa and others*, 1996 Case CCT 17/96, *South African Constitutional Law Review*, LEXIS 20, 38 (1996).
22. Belgian Senate Resolution 1997–1998, Resolution 1–736/3, "Concerning the 1915 genocide of Armenians living in Turkey."
23. Julian Putkowski and Julian Skyes, *Shot at dawn: Executions in World War I by the Authority of the British Army Act* (Barnsley, UK: Wharncliffe, 1989).
24. Daniel L. Schacter. "Memory distortion: History and current status, 1." In *Memory dis-*

tortion: How minds, brains and societies reconstruct the past, Daniel L. Schacter, Ed. (Cambridge, MA: Harvard University Press, 1995).

25. *California v. Franklin,* rev'd, *Franklin v. Duncan,* 884 F.Supp. 1435 (N.D. Cal. 1995). For various accountings of the *Franklin* case, *see* E. Franklin and M. Wright, *Sins of the father* (New York: Crown, 1991), and Lenore Terr, *Unchained memories* (New York: Basic Books, 1994).

26. Amina Memon and Mark Young, "Desperately seeking evidence: The recovered memory debate," *Legal and Criminological Psychology* 2 (1997):1–24.

27. *Demjanjuk v. United States,* 10 F.3d 338 (6th Cir. 1993).

28. See Willem Wagenaar, *Identifying Ivan: A case study in legal psychology* (Cambridge, MA: Harvard University Press, 1988).

29. Marietta Jaeger, "The power and reality of forgiveness: Forgiving the murderer of one's child." In *Exploring forgiveness*, Robert Enright and Joanna North, Eds. (Madison: University of Wisconsin Press, 1998) at 9–14.

30. Suzanne R. Freedman and Robert D. Enright, "Forgiveness as an intervention goal with incest survivors," *Journal of Consulting and Clinical Psychology* 64 (1996):983–992

31. *Campaign against impunity: Portrait and plan of action* (Montreal, Quebec, Canada: International Centre for Human Rights and Democratic Development, 1997).

32. Mark Osiel, *Mass atrocity, collective memory and the law* (New Brunswick, NJ: Transaction, 1997).

33. Ronalth Ochaeta, "Eradicating impunity: The new challenge to democracy and peace in Guatemala." In *Campaign against impunity: Portrait and plan of action* (Montreal, Quebec, Canada: International Centre for Human Rights and Democratic Development, 1997).

34. *Guatemala: Appeals against impunity* (London: Amnesty International, 1997).

35. United Nations High Commission on Human Rights Resolution 1999/34.

36. See David B. Wexler and Bruce J. Winick, *Essays in therapeutic jurisprudence* (Durham, NC: Carolina Academic Press, 1991); David B. Wexler, *Therapeutic jurisprudence: The law as a therapeutic agent* (Durham, NC: Carolina Academic Press, 1990); David B. Wexler and Bruce J. Winick, *Law in a therapeutic key: Developments in therapeutic jurisprudence,* (Durham, NC: Carolina Academic Press, 1996).

37. See chapter 7.

Chapter 2
WHY WE SHOULD PUNISH OLD CRIMES

Should society waive its right to punish if it has failed to act in a timely fashion? The passage of time may change the social and political context in which the accused person finds himself or herself and arguably may even lead to profound changes in the identity of the wrongdoer, but should this affect the institution of punishment? There are many such examples of "prison conversion," some of which are undoubtedly genuine. One case that had such an appearance was that of Karla Faye Tucker, who was sentenced to death in Texas 15 years before her execution date was finally set for the brutal murder of her ex-lover and his companion.[1] By the time of her final appeal, her repentance had led her to become a leader of the prison ministry. Should her profound change affect society's right or obligation to carry out punishment? Opinion in Texas was divided. Opponents of capital punishment pointed to the vindictiveness of executing such a person, arguing that this case convincingly demonstrated the cruelty and futility of the death penalty. Many otherwise enthusiastic supporters of the death penalty also found the case difficult. For them, the stumbling block was the apparent genuineness of the change and the honesty of Tucker's confrontation with her crime. Yet the state carried out the execution. And why should it not, some demanded. Such a homicide is punishable by execution in Texas; the fact that the perpetrator had repented over a period of 15 years was, in this view, irrelevant to the question of punishment.

If society claims the right to punish wrongdoers, then we may reasonably expect it to assert a right to punish distant and recent wrongs. The justifications for punishment, however—and there are numerous theories adduced in support of the right to punish[2]—do not necessarily support the punishment of distant and recent wrongs equally. An argument in favor of an immediate response to a recent wrong may be satisfactory in relation to that particular wrong but unsatisfactory in response to a more distant wrong. The goal that the argument supports may be present in one case but simply absent in the other. In sexual abuse cases, for example, individual deterrence may not be a factor to take into account where the abuse was committed many years previously and was opportunistic, and the perpetrator is now much older and no longer sexually active. However, if the perpetrator is in a position to exploit other victims, then the deterrent aspect of punishment may still be a factor, just as general deterrence may be a factor if the object is to punish the current offender to deter other future offenders. Whether it is right to punish old crimes depends, to a great extent, on the justification for punishment in general. Some of the justifications for punishment are unaffected by the passage of time, whereas others are weakened by its passage. It is interesting to note that although there has been—and continues to be—voluminous academic discussion of the justifications of punishment, the temporal dimension of punishment has been little debated.

This chapter examines why society punishes, including retribution, deterrence, and rehabilitation, and how these goals of punishment are affected by the passage of time in the prosecution of old crimes. Noting that none of these justifications exclude punishment for wrongs of the distant past, the chapter then examines the manner in which the passage of time affects personal identity and notions of responsibility associated with identity.

Much can be understood about the justification for punishment by asking what may initially appear obvious: Why should society punish at all? In one radical view, there is no case for punishment, whether the wrong is recent or otherwise.[3] According to this school of thought, punishment amounts to little more than society hurting itself. The proponents of this theory claim that wrongdoing may be marked by a formal recognition that a wrong has been committed, and this may be accompanied by some act of acknowledgment or apology, but there is no additional need for the infliction of pain on the perpetrator of the wrong. The emphasis in this approach is on taking action to prevent the recurrence of the wrong. This may involve confronting the wrongdoer with what he or she has done, arranging for him or her to address the consequences of his or her acts, or providing education or treatment to help him or her prevent similar action in the future. This approach has no room for the infliction of a measured response in the form of the infliction of pain on the offender.

Although this approach might seem ill-suited for a complex urban society, it finds acceptance in segments of our own judicial system. Consider the philosophy underlying the juvenile justice system. Before the creation of a separate juvenile justice system in the United States in the late 19th century, juvenile crimes were prosecuted in adult court.[4] The juvenile justice system sought to replace punishment with rehabilitation, viewing a system designed merely to punish juvenile offenses as not serving the national interest. Although this distinction between juvenile and adult offenders has become less vivid today in the face of increasingly violent juvenile crime, society still retains the notion that juveniles should be provided with an array of treatment services that it does not furnish for adult offenders.

Nonetheless, particularly in the case of adult offenses, there are profound reasons for opposing the antipunishment position. One cogent argument against this therapeutic vision of the criminal justice system is that to regard crime as a matter of pathology justifies intervention on the basis of what a person might do in the future and not of what that person has done. It is evident that this has nothing to do with desert, and in this respect, it fails to respond to our fundamental intuition that punishment must in some sense be deserved.[5] Apart from any theoretical considerations, the distance that separates this rejection of punishment from the actual practice of society is unbridgeably vast. Every human society uses some form of punishment, formal or informal, and it is inconceivable that a system that categorically rejects any punishment would meet with any degree of public support. Replacing punishment with some form of bureaucratic, nonpunitive response threatens to lead to a society that would be brutish.[6] The withdrawal of punishment appears likely to result in a sharp increase in antisocial behavior, as has happened in those societies (e.g., Somalia in the 1990s),[7] in which the state ceased to enforce any system of criminal law. Society therefore needs to punish, even if its only justification is the need to limit the extent to which crime interferes in the day-to-day conduct of people's lives. There is more to the justification for punishment than this pragmatic need to deter wrongdoing, however. At a very deep level, we are aware of the morally significant nature of punitive behavior, and we draw on a variety of philosophical theories to justify the infliction of what amounts to a considerable measure of pain.

Punishment as Retribution

Retributive theories argue that the infliction of punishment is a duty and that wrongdoers deserve to be punished, whatever the cost and effects of such punishment. The concept has a long pedigree, appearing in the biblical injunction "an eye for an eye, a tooth for a tooth." It is, however, important to distinguish retribution from revenge, which is a separate notion that is more difficult to justify. *Retribution* seeks to redress the moral balance that is "disturbed" by the commission of a crime through the infliction of punishment. *Revenge,* by contrast, satisfies the urge to inflict suffering on those who have wronged us. Revenge has few supporters, at least in the legal discourse, whereas retribution is a morally defensible position and is the most widely accepted justification for punishment in the United States. It is, however, a complex notion. The nature of the moral balance that retribution seeks to restore is not immediately clear, nor is it clear how this balance is corrected through punishing the wrongdoer.

How can the infliction of punishment annul the wrong that has been done to the victim of the wrongful act? From different quarters, victims often express a similar doubt about the restorative possibilities of punishment. A common Jewish observation about the Holocaust is that, even in the face of trials of war criminals and German apologies, "Only the dead can forgive." Sexual abuse victims often echo the view that nothing will ever be the same again. In the words of one victim of the sexual abuser, Rudolph Kos,

> I will never forgive you for the childhood you stole from me. . . . It is that core thinking that has tormented my life. . . . Because of you, the depth of my pain has been so unbearable that many times life has not been worth living. It disgusts me to think my childhood was sacrificed for your moments of pleasure.[8]

The wrong has been committed, the damage has been suffered, and as the victim appears to suggest, no amount of suffering by the wrongdoer will undo the harm. This is a bleak conclusion.

There may be, however, a sense in which we can make the notion of the moral balance more intelligible. When a person is wronged, that person suffers harm. Some harms may, of course, be canceled by the payment of compensation; the victim of a theft who receives the monetary value of his property may well feel that the harm has been annulled. This is distinct from punishment, though. The thief who is obliged to restore stolen property is not punished by this, even if the victim's losses are redressed. Returning art stolen by the Nazis during World War II to the rightful owners may go some way to restore the moral imbalance occasioned by that loss, but it is not punishment of those responsible for the wrongful taking.

Compensation and punishment are distinct concerns. Yet the infliction of punishment on the wrongdoer may nonetheless act to restore the victim's sense of fairness or justice. "I suffered, and now the person who made me suffer is himself suffering" is a sentiment that may bring some degree of satisfaction to some victims, even if not to all victims. If this is the "moral balance" of which retribution speaks, then it has at least some grounding in theories of human psychology.

We may scrutinize this intuition by testing it against the feelings—or what we might imagine to be the feelings—of one who has suffered substantial harm at the hands of a wrongdoer who is apprehended and sentenced to a lengthy term of imprisonment. Consider the case of a war criminal's victim who has been tortured in an internment camp. The camp is liberated, and a sadistic guard, who had brutalized and murdered those under his charge, is brought to justice. The former prisoner is now told that his guard is in a cell, himself incarcerated just as he incarcerated others.

It can be misleading to attribute to others sentiments that we think they might hold. In fact, some who suffer wrong may derive no satisfaction from the punishment of the wrongdoer, but there are undoubtedly many who do. It is therefore possible that the former inmate would express a feeling of satisfaction that the guard should be imprisoned; he might be expected to say "This is fair; this is just." Moreover, even if we cannot be sure about the feelings of the victim, we may at least be confident about how we, as outside observers, might feel about the scene described above. It would be an understandable reaction to think that somehow the ideal of justice in human affairs had been served by visiting punishment on one who had committed such acts.

This satisfaction, it must be admitted, is open to the criticism that it is really no more than a primitive belief in a form of moral symmetry in which an evil deed deserves an evil response. Such a response may be crude in the extreme, and may pay no attention to considerations of intention or accident. The child who destroys another child's property to "repay" the other for breaking his own demonstrates this form of symmetrical response. Primitive it may be, of course, but it could be argued that what is happening here is that a sense of justice is asserting itself, even if inappropriately and indiscriminately. This sense may be developed and refined, becoming an important component of our concept of society.

Retributive punishment may also act as a psychological balm for the victim of the wrong. There are two sets of interests harmed by the commission of crime: the interests of society and the interests of the individual. Both parties—the individual victim and the larger society—may be mollified by the knowledge that the wrongdoer has been punished. This justification for punishment in which its effects are taken into account is consequentialist. Punishment makes people feel better (in this view), and that is a legitimate reason for inflicting it.

There are further aspects of the retributive position that will be considered later; at this point it will be instructive to see how the retributive arguments already marshaled are affected by the passage of time. At first blush, there would seem to be little reason why the fact that a wrong was committed in the distant past should preclude punishment. Punishment is required to "undo" the wrongful act, and until this happens we must presume that the balance remains out of kilter. Even if the victim has forgotten about the wrong or is dead, society must nonetheless give wrongdoers their desert.

The consequences of this rigid position seems absurd when applied to a minor wrong that occurred many years ago. Consider a case where the wrong in question is a minor theft, perhaps the stealing of an inexpensive book. Let us say that Roger takes the book when he is a young man of 19 years. Forty years later, when he is almost 60 years old, his crime is detected. Should Roger be punished for what he did four decades ago? The strict retributionist might be expected to say that for those 40 years the moral balance has been disturbed by the unpunished theft and that the reasons that would have justified punishment 40 years ago are every bit as potent now as they were then.

This rigid insistence on an exact moral tally may be challenged on a number of grounds. At a purely practical level, it is open to the criticism that it is simply a waste of time. If every minor old wrong were to be resurrected for punishment, we would occupy a great part of our time in censuring others—and ourselves. There are practical limits to our ability to take account of all wrongs. If we were to dwell on every past wrong, major and minor, then our lives would simply be too cluttered —and morose—to leave room for our present affairs and projects. This is not to say that we should be forgetful of those wrongs that should be remembered; some wrongs are so significant that we need to remind ourselves of them to remain vigilant against their recurrence. For example, there are compelling arguments that we should not forget the massive wrong of slavery that continues to shape relations between the descendants of those who enslaved and the descendants of those who were en- slaved. These arguments about how we should account for past wrongs also shape our discussion about affirmative action programs to respond to past racial wrongs. The same arguments can be made about not forgetting the great wrongs of the earlier part of the 20th century, such as the terror of Stalinist Russia or the Holocaust, even if the number of those who are alive who actually experienced them diminishes with the years. The remembrance of these major wrongs should not paralyze us, but it might be argued that there is a duty to keep these matters in mind.

Apart from these pragmatic reasons, there is a principled argument that may serve to limit retributive punishment in cases of old wrongs. Retribution is justified on the grounds that it is the adjustment or "correction" of a loss that the victim has suffered. How does the passage of time affect this loss? Will it be canceled after a period, or does the loss remain indefinitely on some metaphysical ledger page until it is annulled?

There is an intuition that some wrongs should be removed from the page by the passage of time because time helps victims to recover. Thus, if Jill steals Ruth's new car, Ruth moves from being a person who enjoys the benefit of new vehicle own- ership to being a person who lacks enjoyment of that benefit. She is subjected to inconvenience and, possibly, some financial loss (the magnitude of which may turn on considerations such as her economic status and employment), while Jill enjoys the advantage of having a new car. This state of affairs, however, will not last forever. In time, Ruth will recover from her loss. She may receive an insurance payment or, even if she does not, she may buy another car. Even if Ruth lacked insurance or the ability to buy another car, at some point the car would have ceased to work and would have become a liability rather than an asset. To use an accounting metaphor, the loss that Ruth suffered is eventually written off and, some time later, the fact that Ruth suffered the loss may make no difference to her overall financial position. She is thus returned to where she was.

The same argument may apply to the nonfinancial loss that the theft involves. At the time of the discovery of the theft and for a period thereafter, Ruth may feel angry and aggrieved. In the usual case, however, her sense of loss or hurt will eventually pass. With the passage of time, she is likely to stop dwelling on the wrong that has been done her and get on with her life without further thought to what happened. In due course, she may even forget about the theft altogether and may only remember if reminded of it. In this respect, too, she is restored to where she was before the theft occurred.

Just as the victim's position may be restored to what it was prior to the theft, so too with the passage of time the thief may be restored to a pre-advantage position.

If Jill is no longer enjoying the car or the fruits of its sale, then the difference that the theft made to her position may be slight or even nonexistent. In these circumstances, the contemplation of her position does not always give rise to a sense of injustice, as it would if she were still enjoying her ill-gotten gain. There may be a sense of injustice based on the fact that the wrongdoer has avoided punishment, but that is based on considerations quite distinct from those of loss and gain.

The argument for retribution is weakened when the passage of time restores the victim to her pre-accident position. Stolen books or cars are a relatively minor matter, however, in the spectrum of the harms addressed by the criminal justice system. The same analysis may yield very different results when applied to a more serious crime. The reason for this lies in the persistence of the harm where the loss is great. So, for example, a person who is permanently damaged by an assault carries that damage and is limited by it, throughout the rest of his or her life. In cases in which a person is raped or subjected to sexual abuse, again the loss may be expected to register for a considerable period, in many cases for life. In some cases there may be no recovery; thus, on these grounds, the loss should be corrected, even if the opportunity to do so presents itself only years later.

The persistence of loss is most evident in cases in which human life is taken. We can understand how the loss endures in cases such as the murder of civil rights leaders in the South during the early 1960s. Many of these murders were either not prosecuted—sometimes inexplicably—or their prosecution resulted in hung juries. For example, Byron De La Beckwith was eventually convicted in 1994 of the murder of Medgar Evers, which took place 31 years earlier.[9] His conviction came about after new evidence surfaced. A similar case was the murder of Vernon Dahmer, referred to in chapter 1; again, we can readily see why many people wanted proceedings to be brought even after decades had passed.

The taking of life is so significant, then, that crimes of homicide are typically never barred by statutes of limitation.[10] Police practice reflects this concern; the discovery of human remains will inevitably be investigated very closely, even if the death occurred many years previously. Community sentiment also frequently points in this direction. The families of those who have been killed are often loathe to abandon ideas of retribution, no matter how long ago the crime took place. The philosophy of retribution, possibly more than any other theory of punishment, takes into account these real and deeply held feelings.

Punishment, in this respect, may be an affirmation of moral community, a social ritual that binds such a community together. Punishment asserts that the wrongdoer is a member of the community and subject to its rules. It is a social ritual, a necessary response to an act that challenges the notion of community. As such, it will be necessary to carry out punishment, even if the immediate harm or hurt to an individual has faded. In addressing this point, Andreas Oldenquist, one exponent, emphasized that the practice of the social ritual of retributive punishment may appear to have nothing to do with utility: "The pursuit of Adolph Eichmann, Joseph Mengele, and other Nazis in their dotage, tending their rose gardens in South America, makes no utilitarian sense whatsoever. They will not do their crimes again, nor would punishment deter others."[11] Other community-based justifications for punishment stress its re-integrative aspect. To punish the criminal, in this view, is to bring the criminal back into the community from which he has alienated himself. Punishment, then, becomes a form of compliment to the wrongdoer, even if it is a compliment that may not always be appreciated.[12]

Many modern defenders of retribution find themselves uncomfortable with what they see as the embarrassingly vague notion of moral balance. They prefer to identify the denunciation of the crime as the purpose of retribution. A wrong has been committed, and now, in exacting retribution, we denounce the wrong. If anyone is in any doubt as to the moral quality of the act, let them now look on the suffering of the perpetrator. Punishment here is expressive: It articulates society's antipathy for the wrong that was done.

The idea that punishment is a public denunciation of wrongdoing has a lengthy pedigree. It was espoused by Kant, in a passage that might be considered to be typical of his tendency to carry an idea to somewhat extreme lengths. Kant suggested that a community abandoning a desert island would be obliged to execute the last murderer in its prison rather than merely leave him behind to a solitary life on the island to avoid being associated with the crime that he had committed.[13] The act of punishment expresses a moral distancing from the crime, the wrongfulness of which is underlined by the otherwise apparently vindictive execution. Modern exponents of denunciation are likely to feel squeamish about this example, but their position is still that by punishing wrongdoers, we manifest our disapproval of the wrongful act and express this both to the victim and to society as a whole. This denunciation addresses both the needs of victim and of society. The victim is shown that the harm he has suffered is both recognized and denounced. Society is shown that its rules are being affirmed and strengthened: The legitimacy of the rule is spelled out by the very fact that there is a response to the rule's infringement.

One might argue that the measure of punishment should not matter in this view —what matters is the fact of punishment—but the measure of punishment does play an important role in that it goes to demonstrate the seriousness with which the conduct is viewed. A severe punishment sends a forceful and unambiguous message condemning the conduct in question; a lenient punishment correspondingly sends a message that although the conduct is wrong, the wrong is not substantial. Accordingly, if there is no punishment at all, then the message conveyed is that the rule does not matter to society and may be ignored. Lenient punishments are often viewed by victims or their relatives as condoning the wrong. This has been a frequent reaction in the past to the lenient sentences imposed on those responsible for sexual offenses committed against women.

The denunciatory justification of punishment has attracted considerable support in recent years. For Joel Feinberg, a philosopher who has elaborated an influential liberal theory of criminal justice, punishment serves an expressive function.[14] When we punish, not only do we make what he calls an "authoritative disavowal" of the wrongful conduct, but we also vindicate the criminal law. Punishment shows that society means what it says about the prescribed conduct; it emphasizes that there has been more than a mere technical breach of a rule. Not to punish a wrong, then, is to convey the message that the wrong is something about which society does not really care. Feminists have argued that the criminal justice system's response to rape is a poignant example of this absence of care.[15]

Like Feinberg, Robert Nozick regarded communication of value as an essential feature of the process of punishment.[16] In punishing a wrongdoer, argued Nozick, society is "connecting" the offender with the correct values that the person has failed to observe. The offender is obliged to appreciate that what he has done is wrong and is obliged to undergo a process that, to all intents and purposes, "rubs his nose" in the offense. Nozick did not explain in any detail what it is to be "connected" with the correct values, but he did emphasize that the suffering implicit in punishment makes it impossible for the wrongdoer to be as pleased with what he did as he would otherwise have been.

This feature of Nozick's argument is tantalizing. If it means that something is taken from the wrongdoer (the enjoyment of the fruits of the wrongdoing or the satisfaction over what was done), then the theory begins to look similar to the traditional retributive call for the redressing of an imbalance of interests. The wrongdoer obtains an advantage over others by acting as he does; unlike the offender, others are obliged to observe the limitations of the law, whereas the wrongdoer, by contrast, obtains a benefit that would normally be denied him. An alternative reading of Nozick's argument is that "wiping the smile off the criminal's face" underscores the seriousness of the prohibition that he has flouted. In this respect, it is a straightforward denunciatory justification.

There is another communicative function that retribution may perform. According to Jean Hampton, when we punish we assert the value of the person who has been the victim of the wrong.[17] She argued that in punishing the criminal, society defeats him and re-establishes the relative value of wrongdoer and victim. The wrongdoer is shown to be a person about whom people care little—the offender is sent to prison, fined, or placed on probation, whereas the victim is given our sympathy and, therefore, ends up in a better position than the wrongdoer. This infliction of pain on the perpetrator of the harm demonstrates that society is concerned about the wrong done to the victim, and that it is prepared to mark this by going to the trouble—and expense—of inflicting punishment.

An influential contemporary justification of punishment as a communicative act has been attempted by Anthony Duff, who sees the act of communication as being addressed not so much to society in general, but to the wrongdoer. The justification of punishment, in his view, lies in the fact that it gives the wrongdoer the chance to make penance for the wrong. It forces the wrongdoer to confront the message that is being addressed to him, namely, that the act was wrong and that the offender should accept its wrongfulness.

> We owe it to every moral agent to treat him as one who can be brought to reform and redeem himself—to keep trying, however vainly, to reach the good that is in him, and to appeal to his capacity for moral understanding and concern.[18]

Punishment is therefore for the criminal's benefit: It confirms his autonomy and gives him the chance to become reconciled with the moral values of the society he inhabits. Of course, the wrongdoer may not wish to achieve this reconciliation—and in particular may not wish to achieve it through the experience of hard treatment at the hands of the state—in which case the imposition of punishment becomes paternalistic.

Critics of denunciatory theories have pointed out that actual punishment need not figure in the equation; the state could quite easily establish a means of showing its disapproval of wrongs either by stating its abhorrence of a particular wrongdoing or by treating the victim in such a way as to show sympathy. Neither of these would involve inflicting punishment on the offender, yet each would amount to a denunciation. However, denunciatory gestures such as these could easily escape the perpetrator, who could either be unaware of them or could—and this is quite likely—cynically be indifferent to them. Denunciation should be directed not only to society at large, but specifically to the wrongdoer. Punishment draws the offender's attention to society's disapproval of his act in a way that he cannot ignore.

Denunciation is as compatible with the punishment of old wrongs as it is with the punishment of recent ones. The fact that a wrong was committed in the distant past does not mean that we cannot register our disapproval of it, and indeed there is a sense in which a failure to care about the wrongs of the past represents a lack of moral sensitivity. This may seem morally overfastidious, yet if we explore the notion further, it is seen to be morally consistent. No person with any concern for the suffering of others would talk lightly of a major, comparatively recent wrong such as the Holocaust. To say that this event did not matter would strike many as insensitive (at the least) or even as evil. Such large-scale suffering simply cannot leave one cold, just as one cannot be left unmoved by other acts of human brutality of the even more recent past. These events are vivid, to be sure, and our moral reaction to them is correspondingly strong. Consistency, however, would require us to feel the same about events of the more distant past. Surely it would be wrong to feel unmoved by the mistreatment by the Spanish Conquistadors of the peoples of Central America or by the hunting down of the Tasmanian Aborigines by British colonists. Every wrong of this sort involves the same type of human suffering and pain, and one might argue that this suffering deserves the same respect as does more recent suffering. The only thing that distinguishes recent suffering from suffering of the distant past is its vividness.

It would seem absurd, though, for a person in our own times to denounce solemnly the depredations of the Roman Empire or the cruelties of Attila the Hun. Yet it would strike us as distasteful to talk of these events with a smile of glee; if pressed to express a view, we might say that these events involved cruelty or suffering and that it cannot have been pleasant to have been on the receiving end. The real issue is moral impact; events of the very distant past generally have a diminished moral impact on our lives. By contrast, events of the more recent past have a greater impact because they bear on the texture of our own moral lives. This resonance arises from identification with the people involved. It occurs because in some way, even possibly an attenuated way, we engage with some parts of the past and not with others. We may be entitled to ignore the distant wrongs of history because they are simply no longer relevant to us, but if events belong to the morally resonating past, then they form part of our current moral landscape and may require denunciation, compensation, or even punitive action.

This process of engagement with the morally relevant, even if relatively distant past, is illustrated in the contemporary debate over historical reparations. In the United States, as in a number of other countries—principally Australia and New Zealand—the past 3 decades have witnessed a process of acknowledgment of claims that find their basis in wrongs going well back into the 19th century.[19] The claims in question are those made by minority communities who feel that their current situation is disadvantaged by what was done, not necessarily to them personally, but to their forbears. One facet of these claims is the demand for compensation, the argument being that the descendants of those who have been wrongfully deprived of property or who have been denied the chance to compete on equal terms should have their position rectified by being put into the position in which they would otherwise have been. This argument is by no means universally accepted, even if it has persuaded some; we do not intend to become involved in it here. What interests us, though, is the fact that part and parcel of these historical injustice claims is a demand for the recognition and denunciation of a past injustice. In the case of Maori claims in New Zealand, this has been met by a government apology for 19th-century breaches of the Treaty of Waitangi, the pact between the British Crown and its Maori subjects.[20]

If groups of people living in the final years of the 20th century can feel so strongly about what happened in the middle- to late-19th century, it is not surprising that wrongs more recent than these should require denunciation. A major wrong suffered in childhood may be morally relevant for an adult in the closing years of his or her life; in such a case, the need for denunciation may be as strongly felt as if the wrong were a few weeks old. If the victim is dead, the need to denounce may seem less obvious, and yet there are good grounds for arguing that denunciation is still required. The dead may lack certain rights in the normal legal sense, yet how we treat the dead does matter. We regard it as wrong, for example, to ignore testamentary wishes, and in some legal systems it is a civil wrong, actionable in the courts, to defame the dead. We also respect their memory in the moral sense; speaking ill of the dead is considered a wrong, even if it is debatable whether there can be any such thing as a posthumously inflicted harm. There may be good reasons, then, for treating such events as still morally relevant to us; we retain an engagement with those who are dead but whom we remember, and we may wish, then, to pursue wrongs against them out of respect for their memory.

A striking illustration of this desire to redress a wrong for the sake of the memory of the dead is provided by the unsuccessful campaign in the British Parliament to obtain an official posthumous pardon for soldiers executed for desertion and disobedience to orders in World War I.[21] Many of these men, who were given summary trials in the field, might now be diagnosed as suffering from posttraumatic stress disorder. In many cases they were brave soldiers who had been pushed beyond endurance and who had eventually been overcome by the horror of their experiences. Their modern supporters—some, but by no means all, of whom are relatives—feel sufficiently strongly about the memory of those who died over 80 years ago to devote a great deal of time and effort to a posthumous recognition of what they see as a gross injustice.

Past events often bear current moral importance. If there is any role for denunciation, then this role covers all of those events included in the circle of moral recognition. There may be many views on how this circle is to be described. The political use of history means that those wrongs that assist a current claim—whether it is a private claim or a claim by a whole people or community—may well be kept alive in memory. There may be a serious case for the tending of some of these memories, but some degree of skepticism is appropriate here: These wrongs may be used as excuses for thoroughly modern hatreds as in the Balkans or Northern Ireland.

Other Theories of Punishment

For some, punishment is justified only if it leads to a result that is good for society or for the individual. This approach, which justifies rules on the basis of their utility, sees no benefit in punishing wrongdoers simply because they have committed a wrong; this punishment achieves nothing and may amount to no more than the infliction of pointless pain. What justifies punishment, according to utilitarian thinking, is deterrence (which benefits society) or rehabilitation (which benefits the individual and society).

Unlike retributive theories, deterrence theories of punishment are empirically testable. A central claim of these theories is that threatening a sanction deters people from committing wrongs because the gain they see in committing the wrong is rendered unattractive by the penalty. This may operate at a specific level, in that the offender who has been punished once will be less likely to repeat his offense because he knows what awaits him if he does, and at a general level, in that others will be disinclined to offend in the face of punishment.

Deterrent theories accord with what we think we know about human behavior. The empirical evidence, however, is less than clear, and there remains considerable doubt as to the efficacy of deterrence. Some criminologists claim that the available empirical evidence points to the efficacy of punishment as a deterrent[22]; others question the extent to which the imposition of severe penalties makes any difference to patterns of antisocial conduct. The impact on the offender of prosecuting an old crime may be difficult to justify in deterrent terms. If, for example, the reason that a person has not been prosecuted for the old crime is that he has avoided the authorities by living a law-abiding life over the past 30 years, that may seem good evidence that he is unlikely to begin offending now. Moreover, many of the crimes committed by such people may be specific to the context in which they found themselves at the time. This is often pointed out in respect to crimes committed in circumstances of civil disturbance or war; an 18-year-old conscript who shot a civilian is unlikely to repeat the offense as a 70-year-old veteran.

The general deterrence argument in such cases, however, is far stronger. The fact that a particular accused may be unlikely to re-offend does not detract from the deterrent value of punishing the offender to deter others. The fact that the crime is an old one lends force to the deterrent. In punishing a wrongdoer many years after the offense, society effectively emphasizes that it will not give up its pursuit of those who violate its laws. Insisting on tardy punishment stresses the inescapability of punishment, a message that may register with other potential offenders.

This argument can be applied credibly in the case of both war criminals and those who commit sexual offenses against children, two of the main categories of wrongdoers affected by the old crimes issue. In the case of war criminals, prosecuting war crimes even long after the cessation of hostilities vividly emphasizes to soldiers that they cannot rely on the abnormality of war conditions to mask their offenses; war crimes will survive the armistice and haunt the perpetrator in peacetime. In the case of those who commit sexual offenses against children, instituting prosecution many years after the event makes clear that even if the crime is undisclosed during the childhood of the victim, society may not regard it as too late to do anything about it. In practice, there will be restrictions on this. Statutes of limitations impose a time limit on the bringing of charges, and this may effectively cut off any redress open to the adult who was abused as a child. These rules are explored at greater length in chapter 4.

The other utilitarian goals of incapacitation and rehabilitation apply less clearly to the punishment of old crimes. Indeed, there will often be an indirect correlation between the passage of time and the relevance of incapacitation or rehabilitation of the offender. Incapacitation is less likely to be relevant when, owing to the passage of time and the aging process, the accused is no longer actively involved in the offending conduct.[23] Rehabilitation might in some cases be relevant in the case of an old crime, but this depends on the age of the accused. It is questionable whether punishment is going to make an aged offender into a more useful citizen or a better person.

Our brief survey of the main justifications for punishment suggests that there is nothing in the main strands of retributive or utilitarian theories that excludes the punishment of wrongs from the distant past. We endorse no particular theory of punishment; our aim has merely been to show that there is no general reason to consider the prosecution of old crimes to be pointless in terms of the commonly voiced justifications of punishment, although the passage of time may ameliorate its fervor. In terms of these theories, then, society is fully entitled to punish the wrongs of the past. What remains to be seen is if there are any other principled reasons why society should not do so. In pursuit of this question we now turn to what may seem like an obscure philosophical excursus but which, in fact, is very relevant to our main inquiry: Is the person whom we are punishing the same person who committed the crime? This is a fundamental question for the prosecution of any crime; in this context, though, it raises puzzling issues of personal identity of the sort that normally does not concern the criminal courts.

Personal Identity: Is One the Same Person as One Was 20 Years Ago?

When people reflect on their past, it is not uncommon for them to say something like "I was not the same person then as I am today." This might well be said with remorse as an expression of regret that the abilities or attributes of youth have been lost, or it might be said as an expression of an excuse that distances us from youthful indiscretions. If we feel regret for having done in the past something that we would not do today, then the claim that we are not the same person is a way of distancing ourselves from some wrongful act.

The statement might mean more than one thing. In one sense, it is a protestation of change. The maker of the statement tells us that we should not consider him or her to be the sort of person who would today do such a thing. Karla Faye Tucker, the repentant, model prisoner mentioned at the beginning of this chapter, claimed that she was not the same person as the drug-addicted prostitute who murdered a man and a woman with a pick ax. Those who claim that they have changed ask us to judge their character by what they are now rather than by what they were in the past. "I may have been intolerant then, but I no longer am," or "I may then have been the sort of person to falsify my expenses claims, but I no longer am." The statement, in this sense, may also be forward-looking, in which the individual asks that his or her future conduct should not be predicated on the basis of what has been done before.

An alternative reason for making such a claim is that the current person has nothing to do with that past identity. This is a claim to an excuse, intended to expunge the acts of the past person from the moral account of the present person.

This amounts to a denial of responsibility for past acts that challenges the way in which we normally attribute blame. There is a strong presumption in favor of holding the historical actor liable for what he has done. So strong is this view, that it would strike many as absurd to excuse people on the basis that their identity had in some way changed. There is something in our intuitions as to changes in personal identity that needs to be examined, however, even if we seem set for the conclusion that personal identity claims should provide little comfort for those accused of old crimes.

Philosophers have long been intrigued by the apparently simple question of whether a person has the same identity over time or whether the changes wrought by time may be sufficient to change overall identity.[24] Is the person in the cradle as an infant the same person on the deathbed at the age of 90? Our immediate response is likely to be that of course it is the same person. Although individual cells die and replace themselves, there is clearly a degree of bodily continuity across the years. In particular, the brain is recognizably the same organ, even if some changes occur in brain structure as a person gets older. The infant and the adult are therefore one and the same organism, even if there are obvious differences.

This observation is based on physical continuity, and is undoubtedly true, in the context of physical identity. To say that body of the 90-year-old is the same body as that of the infant is unobjectionable, but this is not necessarily the same as saying that the body is the person. Personhood is a somewhat larger conception than bodily existence, and it may be that even if the body remains the same, there may be reasons why we should regard the person as having changed. The statement "I am not the same person" does not strike us as meaningless. There does appear to be an important respect in which the notion of the person is not entirely dependent on the notion of the body, even if, in the normal case, the person and the body are inextricably linked. An example of the division made between the person and the body is provided by the way in which personhood is seen to be absent in those who have suffered an irreversible loss of consciousness and cessation of upper brain function. The person who was the patient before this disaster may simply no longer be there in the eyes of those who knew him, and the *absence of the person* may be the term that they use to describe the change that has occurred. This dichotomy between the body and the person underlies the debate about terminating life support for those individuals in a persistent vegetative state whose bodies no longer seem to house the people who once inhabited them.

Some writers on personal identity have been willing to relegate the continuity of bodily identity to a secondary role, attributing greater importance to memory as the cement of continuity in personal identity.[25] The fact that I currently remember doing something on my birthday last year is what makes me the same person as the one who acted on my birthday last year. If, by contrast, I forget having done what was done on my birthday last year, then I do not share an identity with the person who acted at that point. There are numerous objections to this memory thesis, but there is much to be said for this notion that remembering is an important part of personal identity.

Would a memory-focused theory of personal identity allow us to say of a person who forgets that he did something criminal in the distant past that the person is not the same one who committed the act? The answer to this question depends on the context in which the issue is framed. In each case the same physical body acted, to be sure, but the same consciousness is not present in each case. A person consists not just of a physical body but is also a center of consciousness. This consciousness has an identity over time, without which it is no more than a mere succession of fleeting mental states. When we talk of a person, then, we mean, first and foremost, this consciousness in all its dimensions. We mean the historical context in which it is embedded, its experiences, and its dispositions. To this list one might add the concept of character, which consists not only of dispositions but also of abilities to control dispositions.

In everyday life we make only incidental, and hazy, distinctions between the nonphysical person and the body. When this distinction is made, however, it is revealing. A reflex act, for example, is not one for which we will be held responsible. Nor will the action of a sleepwalker be one for which he will be held accountable; "he" simply did not do it. The bearer of responsibility is not the actor's body, it is the person represented by that body. If it is the person as a site of consciousness that counts for purposes of blaming or praising, then there must be some link established between the current consciousness (which is the object of blame) and the consciousness responsible for the earlier act. Yet how is this link to be established? One way of doing so would be to say that they both occupy the same space or are dependent on the same brain. But should this fact make them identical? Consciousness is notoriously difficult to define, but whether it is a physical event indistinguishable from the electrical activity that creates it, or whether it is a nonphysical phenomenon that is merely dependent on—but not the same thing as—brain matter, it clearly has a strongly transitory nature. Memory links states of consciousness with one another, and this provides the sense of context within which consciousness exists.[26] This context goes toward making up the personal identity on which personhood is founded. We remember previous states of consciousness and realize that these states were the precursors of the current state of consciousness. They were precursors in more than a merely accidental sense, however. The features of the earlier state of consciousness have a bearing on the self of the time, and this in turn affects the later self.

For some writers on this issue, what provides identity over time is psychological connectedness.[27] This is a link between mental states, a link that may be established not only by the overlapping of successive states of mind but also by the foreseeability of accountability in the future for what one does today.[28] This connectedness need not be strong: We are prepared to accept that identity exists when the links are considerably attenuated.[29] Severe disruption, however, may be sufficient to break the link between earlier and later selves or might occur in cases in which advanced dementia (as in the later stages of Alzheimer's disease) creates a gulf between earlier and current mental states.[30] The example of the person with dementia, in fact, proves to be a useful means of capturing the grounds for our intuition that it would be wrong—indeed cruel—to hold the self with dementia liable for the actions of the predementia self; not only has the memory disappeared in such a case, but the entire sense of self may be eroded and dramatically changed. In advanced dementia the sense of self is detached from all the familiar anchoring points of identity—family, sense of place, and long-established interests and preferences. This is severance of a quite different order from the change that one might normally expect between the 20-year-old man and his 70-year-old later self. In the latter case, even if interests and attitudes have changed, it should be possible to detect connections, or overlap of mental states, even if there has been a degree of memory loss. In the case of the person with dementia, there is, in a very real sense, a new person.

The most obvious link, though, between our current state of consciousness and states of consciousness in the past is through the body that consciousness inhabits. For most people, this will be the deciding feature in attributing identity between successive states of consciousness. We assume that, for example, the "Stella person" in Stella's body today is the same as the person in Stella's body a year ago. This may be so, and in most cases there are likely to be enough of the contextual links mentioned above to make this true. If Stella has undergone experiences that significantly weaken or obliterate the links between her current and past states of consciousness, however, then in an important sense this identity is missing. In such a case we may reasonably say that it is a different person—in the sense of a distinctive state of consciousness—occupying a physically continuous body.

If we accept that the change in a person is so significant that the current self has nothing in common with the past self, then it seems reasonable to say that the person is different. The current self might remember the past self but does that make them identical? Memory of an event itself is surely not what makes for responsibility for that event; what counts for responsibility is authorship by an identifiable agent. The crux of the question then is whether it makes sense to say that in some cases, the agent has so changed that the authorship of acts performed by the historical predecessor of that person (the former self) has nothing to do with the current person. This has no bearing on mercy or forgiveness; it is a defense of the "It was not me" variety.

Although there are undoubtedly arguments in favor of recognizing this profound form of change, there are also perhaps more telling arguments against it. The most cogent of these is that the principle of accountability would be hopelessly compromised if people were to be allowed to deny agency in this way. If we are to be held responsible for our acts—and we must be—then we need a notion of a continuous self underlying legal responsibility. To allow disclaimers of agency based on inner change would be to introduce an impossible note of uncertainty into our dealings with one another. If we could deny authorship of a legal act—a contract, for example—on the grounds that it was another self that signed the agreement, then business and commercial affairs would become uncertain. All our social dealings, including praise and reward, are based on the notion of a unified and continuing personhood embodied in a relatively unchanging fleshly envelope. We may think that we can re-invent ourselves, but for the purposes of the attribution of responsibility, re-invention is irrelevant.

This is not to say that the idea of personal change should not have some bearing on punishment. Even if we reject the claim that a wrongdoer has become a different person, the fact of change may have a bearing on the justification of inflicting punishment on him or her. The argument for retribution is certainly not affected by this, as retribution is not concerned with the attitude of the wrongdoer at the time of punishment. Other forward-looking justifications for punishment are, however, affected. A changed person will probably represent no danger to society and, thus, does not require to have the wrongfulness of the act forcefully brought home. There is no point in reminding the perpetrator of the pain caused to others; if the wrongdoer has changed in a positive way, he or she should be well aware of it.

Change, then, must be limited to a marginal role in matters of responsibility.

Where it comes into its own is as a trigger of forgiveness, which is the subject of the following chapter. It is easier to forgive a changed person than it is to forgive one who has not changed. Indeed, to withhold forgiveness from a changed person seems churlish. Yet when convicted murderers find religion on death row and become, by all accounts, "different people," they may find that the conversion fails to persuade those who exercise the power of clemency. Justice, it would seem, is blind in more ways than one.

Punishment and Age

In many cases when a long time has elapsed between the commission of the crime and the apprehension of the wrongdoer, prosecuting authorities will be faced with the prospect of an aged defendant. This has obviously been the case with any prosecutions brought in the last decade of the 20th century relating to crimes committed during World War II. The former French civil servant, Maurice Papon, convicted in 1998 of complicity in forced removals of Jews in Vichy France, was 87 years old at the time of his conviction.[31] Erich Priebke, the German officer charged with shooting over 300 Italian civilians in a reprisal for partisan killing of German soldiers, was brought to court at the age of 82.[32] The defendants, or potential defendants, investigated under the British War Crimes Act of 1991, which gave courts in the United Kingdom the power to try war crimes committed in German-occupied territories between 1939 and 1945, were similarly all in their late 70s or 80s.[33] Indeed, one of the few English prosecutions initiated under this legislation had to be abandoned because the defendant had senile dementia.

General Augusto Pinochet, the former Chilean dictator from 1973 until 1990, was arrested in London in 1998 at the request of a Spanish court seeking his extradition on numerous charges of torture and murder. The case involved a difficult and controversial issue of jurisdiction, and in particular it raised the question of whether a former head of state was immune to criminal charges arising from acts he committed while in office. In the end, the British courts confirmed that diplomatic immunity did not cover torture and murder, which were beyond the scope of the legitimate acts of a head of state.[34] This enabled the British government to make Pinochet available for extradition, a decision that was greeted with enthusiasm by human rights groups, by survivors of the Pinochet regime, and by the families of people who had been killed by Pinochet's forces. In making the announcement that the British government would not oppose extradition, the Home Secretary stressed that the length of time that had elapsed since the commission of many of the offences in question—25 years—was irrelevant.[35] Also, it appeared, was the general's age: 83 at the time of his arrest.

The Pinochet case is a good case to test the role that age may play in these matters. One response to the demands for his trial might be to ask what point is there in prosecuting an elderly man. Assuming that the extradition process in such a case might take up to a year and that the trial itself, as well as any subsequent appeal, takes another year or more, if he lived that long, any punishment would be likely to begin when the defendant reached 85 or 86. At that age, Pinochet's life expectancy would be short, and if a sentence were imposed that corresponded to the murders charged, it is reasonable to assume that Pinochet would die in prison. Of course, effectively depriving people of their remaining years is not unusual: Many prisoners are given sentences that allow little hope of release. So it could be argued that there is no injustice here; admittedly any prison sentence will have much harsher implications for one who has a short time left to live, but a harsh sentence might simply reflect the seriousness of the crime.

As events turned out, the question of whether it would be oppressive for General Pinochet to face trial in a Spanish court was rendered academic by the conclusion of the British government that his deteriorating physical health made it inappropriate to continue with extradition proceedings.[36] General Pinochet was allowed to return to Chile in early 2000, although he was faced there with demands for the withdrawal of his immunity from prosecution. The expensive and controversial proceedings surrounding the Pinochet case underline the inherent risk in attempting to bring aged defendants to justice. Given the high risk of dementia that a person over age 80 faces, it should not be surprising in any particular case that fitness to face trial might become an issue.

If we are uneasy about prosecuting elderly defendants, then the source of our unease must be located in something other than discomfort over the prospect that the defendant's remaining years will be spent in prison. The real objection to punishing elderly people must reside in what we feel about them as people. In general, we seek to treat elderly people with a degree of consideration that we might not necessarily accord to others. We take into account their physical frailty and their possible inability to look after themselves. We understand their vulnerability and appreciate that the world may at times seem to them to be a confusing and daunting place. In other words, unless we are very unsympathetic, we treat elderly people in some ways as special, in the same way we treat very young people as special. This is not to say that we are not occasionally callous toward elderly people, condescending to them or paternalistically ignoring their own preferences. Elderly people are in a sense excluded, sometimes in ways that are hurtful to them.

Even if elderly people are sometimes treated as an embarrassment or an irrelevance, nobody likes the thought of deliberately imposing suffering on them. We react to assaults on elderly people with much the same outrage as we react to assaults on young children; these are acts of particular cruelty because of the defenselessness of the victim. To subject an elderly person to abuse, then, is seen as an act of bullying: There is an inequality between the perpetrator and the victim. But is there any parallel between bullying elderly people and punishing them for their misdeeds? We must separate here a number of distinct factors. We have already considered the personal identity issue and have seen that it plays a role in our thinking about people over the decades. It is possible that one of the reasons why we may be disinclined to call elderly people to account is that we see them as different people from the people they were all those years ago. Some may see the connection between the young man of 20 and the old man of 80 as being just too attenuated, perhaps, to feel comfortable about visiting on the 80-year-old the misdeeds of the 20-year-old. This may be a powerful factor in favor of mitigation, even if we reject, as we have done above, the notion that there should be a formal personal identity defense that actually affects agency. Leaving aside, then, this personal identity issue, we might consider whether, first, calling an elderly person to account is unduly oppressive and, second, if punishing an elderly person is wrong on similar grounds.

There is nothing intrinsically wrong with asking elderly people to account for their actions. To do so is to treat them on the same basis as one treats others, which is their moral right and, provided that they have not suffered memory loss in relation to the incidents in question, they are at no greater disadvantage than anybody else in explaining their actions. It is only if we saw old age as a disability of a general nature, similar to insanity, for example, that we should think it inappropriate. However, one might argue that the mere fact of calling an old person to account is in itself oppressive in that it imposes a burden on the weak and fragile. Old age and its indignities constitute a misfortune. To add yet another misfortune to an existing one seems wrong because it denies the natural sympathy that we feel for those who suffer.

The imposition of punishment, of course, may seem even more like the imposition of an additional burden of suffering. Punishing another who is already suffering seems cruel, and it is our revulsion against this that leads to the early release from prison of those who have a serious illness—a matter discussed in the context of pardon in chapter 5. In such a case we effectively say that the wrongdoer has suffered enough and does not deserve the extra suffering. So it may be that the reason we feel uncomfortable about punishing elderly people is that we regard them as already laboring under a burden, and we feel that to add to that burden would result in their being punished unduly. The fact that the original burden is a natural one, and not a matter of desert, should enter into our calculation, but it does not.

Yet we should proceed with care. If we remove elderly people from the category of those who might be punished, this might seem rather like removing them from the moral community and might be just as insulting as removing them, for example, from the electoral vote. There is a danger that we regard elderly people as "not counting" when people ignore the preferences of elderly people or make decisions as to their welfare without consulting them. Earlier in this chapter we encountered the moral community theory of punishment that stresses that the act of punishing is intended to affirm the wrongdoer's membership in the moral community. Declining to punish elderly people, although perhaps well intentioned, may indicate exclusion rather than inclusion.

In the final analysis, whom we think it appropriate to punish and whom we do not is probably a matter of custom and category. It is probably also an issue that is culturally defined. Previous ages might have thought it wrong to punish women, or at least held that certain punishments (e.g., corporal punishment) should not be inflicted on women. At other times, certain privileged social groups—members of religious orders, nobles, and the like—have been immune to certain punishments. Who is punished, then, might depend on whom we respect or treat as special. Elderly people tend to be in that category, and this might be as important an explanation as any other.

Even if it seems wrong to punish a man in his 80s, there may still be compelling reasons for doing so if nonpunishment denies justice to those whose suffering would otherwise remain unrecognized. Those who called for the punishment of general Pinochet made this point very eloquently. Unless Pinochet were called to account, it was argued, there would be no public declaration that the suffering of the victims was real, that it happened. This acknowledgment may well be sufficiently important to justify prosecuting a man in the last years of his life. Indeed, this logic might be used to support trying a defendant posthumously in some circumstances to obtain a public accounting of massive wrongdoing. Whether this goes too far turns on whether these past acts remain morally relevant.

Endnotes

1. "Face to face with Jesus: After a long and passionate debate, Karla Faye Tucker goes to her death," *Time,* Feb. 16, 1998, at 157.
2. A useful collection of seminal contributions to the punishment debate is Robin Antony Duff and David Garland, Eds., *A reader on punishment* (Oxford, England: Oxford University Press, 1994).
3. Nils Christie, *Limits to pain* (Oslo, Norway: Universitetsforlag, 1981).
4. Loren Warboys and Wilber Shannon, "Mental health issues in juvenile justice." In *Law, mental health and mental disorder*, Bruce D. Sales and Daniel W. Shuman, Eds. (Pacific Grove, CA: Brooks Cole, 1996) at 503–521.
5. This point is discussed by George Sher, *Desert* (Princeton, NJ: Princeton University Press, 1987) at 74.
6. Andrew von Hirsch, *Past or future crimes* (Manchester, England: Manchester University Press, 1985) at 48.
7. *Campaign against impunity: Portrait and plan of action* (Montreal, Quebec, Canada: International Centre for Human Rights and Democratic Development, 1997).
8. "Kos abuse victim says he can 'never forgive,'" *The Fort Worth Star–Telegram,* Apr. 2, 1998, *Thursday Arlington AM Edition, News,* at 17.
9. David Holmberg, "Civil rights era saw countless killings," *The Palm Beach Post,* Sept. 4, 1994, at 11A.
10. See chapter 4.
11. Andreas Oldenquist, "An explanation of retribution," *Journal of Philosophy* 85 (1988): 404–478, at 404.
12. Eric Reitan, "Punishment and community: The reintegrative theory of punishment," *Canadian Journal of Philosophy* 26(2) (1998):57–81.
13. Immanuel Kant, *The metaphysics of morals* (New York: Cambridge University Press, 1996).
14. Joel Feinberg, *Doing and deserving* (Princeton, NJ: Princeton University Press, 1970).
15. Susan Estrich, *Real rape* (Cambridge, MA: Harvard University Press, 1987).
16. Robert Nozick, *Philosophical explanations* (Cambridge, MA: Harvard University Press, 1981).
17. Jeffrie Murphy and Jean Hampton, *Forgiveness and mercy* (Cambridge, England: Cambridge University Press, 1988) at 125.
18. Robin Antony Duff, *Trials and punishment* (Cambridge, England: Cambridge University Press, 1986) at 266.
19. The issue is discussed by George Sher, "Ancient wrongs and modern rights," *Philosophy and Public Affairs* 10 (1981):3–17.
20. *See* Andrew Sharp, *Justice and the Maori* (Auckland, New Zealand: Oxford University Press, 1997).
21. For a full account, *see* Julian Putkowski and Julian Sykes, *Shot at dawn: Executions in World War I by authority of the British Army Act* (Barnsley, England: Wharncliffe, 1998).
22. See, in general, the discussion in C. L. Ten, *Crime, guilt, and punishment* (Oxford, England: Oxford University Press, 1987) at 7.
23. See Michael Gotfredson and Travis Hirschi, *A general theory of crime* (Stanford, CA: Stanford University Press, 1990), whose analysis reveals an inverted J form that describes the relationship between age and all types of crime.

24. There is an extensive literature on the issue of personal identity. A useful collection is John Perry, Ed., *Personal identity* (Berkeley: University of California Press, 1995). See, also, Sydney Shoemaker and Richard Swinburne, Eds., *Personal identity* (Oxford, England: Blackwell, 1984); Derek Parfit, *Reasons and persons* (Oxford, England: Clarendon Press, 1984); and Jennifer Radden, *Divided minds and successive selves: Ethical issues in disorders of identity and personality* (Cambridge, MA: MIT Press, 1996).

25. For a classic exposition of this position, *see* Herbert Grice, "Personal identity," *Mind* 50 (1941):330–340. *See also* Mrinal Miri, "Memory and personal identity," *Mind* 82 (1973): 1–21.

26. *Id.,* Grice, "Personal identity."

27. See, e.g., Parfit, *Reasons and persons, supra* note 24.

28. Walter Glannon, "Moral responsibility and personal identity," *American Philosophical Quarterly* 35 (1998):231–249.

29. The issue of personal identity is discussed in the context as to surviving competence by Dan Brock and Allan Buchanan, *Deciding for others: The ethics of surrogate decision making* (New York: Cambridge University Press, 1989).

30. Tony Hope, "Personal identity and psychiatric illness," *Philosophy* 37(Suppl.) (1994): 131–143.

31. Arno Klarsfeld, *Papon: Un verdict Français* [Papon: The French verdict] (Paris, France: Ramsay, 1998). See also Bertram Gordon, "Collaboration, retribution, and crimes against humanity: The Touvier, Bousquet, and Papon affairs," *Contemporary French Civilization* 19 (1995): 250.

32. Celestine Bohlen, "Italy opens trial in wartime massacre in Rome," *The New York Times,* Dec. 8, 1995, at A4.

33. Theodor Meron, "International criminalization of internal atrocities," *American Journal of International Law* 89 (1995):554–577.

34. In re Pinochet 1All ER 577 (House of Lords, January 15, 1999).

35. *Id.*

36. Joseph R. Geogory, "World Briefing," *The New York Times,* Late ed.-final, Mar. 7, 2000, Sec. A at 8: "Judge Juan Guzman Tapia requested that the Appeals Court revoke Gen. Augusto Pinochet's immunity so that he can proceed with indictments against the former dictator involving charges of torture, kidnappings and executions. Should the Appeals Court agree, General Pinochet's lawyers can be expected to appeal the decision of the Supreme Court. General Pinochet has been a Senator for Life, a position that grants him broad immunity from prosecution, since 1998."

Chapter 3
FORGIVING THE PAST:
Resentment and Morality

I had gradually begun to realize the existence of the phenomena of reconciliation among chimpanzees. Sometimes the maneuver is fairly obvious. Within minutes of a fight having ended the two former opponents may rush towards each other, kiss, and embrace long and fervently and then proceed to groom each other. But sometimes this kind of emotional contact takes place hours after a conflict. When I observed very carefully, I saw that the tension and hesitancy remained as long as the opponents had not reconciled their differences. Then suddenly the ice would break, and one of the chimpanzees would approach the other.[1]

Wrongdoing can breed resentment. We learn this at an early age and see it in virtually every sphere of our daily lives. The cause of the resentment may be trivial —as in road rage in which one driver attacks another for some minor infraction— or it may be weighty—as in a case in which a parent confronts a person who has harmed his or her child. Our concern is not the physiological processes behind anger, nor are we concerned with sociobiological explanations of its function. We are interested here with the part played by resentment in our moral lives and how it dictates our dealings with those who have wronged us. We accept the reality of the feelings involved and do not question the entitlement to feel wronged over an injustice or injury. What we do question, though, is the extent to which these feelings or emotions should continue to act on us as time distances us from the original wrong.

At what point should we say that the wrong is annulled, and what part should the wronged person play in this process of annulment? This brings us to the question of forgiveness, and its related notion—mercy. In the context of old crimes, the particular question that forgiveness raises is whether the passage of time in itself makes forgiveness an imperative. We sympathize with the resentment of those who have been recently wronged; we are very much less inclined to sympathize with those who have been wronged in the distant past and who have refused to forgive. "You should forgive," we often say. But why? What makes forgiveness a duty?

We begin with an examination of why wrongdoing may breed resentment and the importance that resentment plays in articulating notions of right and wrong. Having recognized the importance of resentment, we consider moral and pragmatic grounds for limiting the intensity and duration of resentment over wrongdoing and when a duty to forgive exists. From here we proceed to address whether, when, and under what conditions to forgive, as well as the role of forgiveness in limiting resentment.

Wrongs and Resentment

When we suffer a wrong at the hands of another, we may experience feelings of resentment. There are other views of the emotion that we experience in these circumstances. In addition to—or instead of—resentment, we may feel indignation.[2] These feelings may arise from our detection of the wrongdoer's ill will toward us. The wrongdoer does not value something about us that we ourselves value. In wronging us, the person treats our interest in being respected by others, our interest in our property, or our interest in our bodily integrity, as being unworthy of his or her respect. In other words, the wrongdoer fails to recognize certain rights that may be very important to the way in which we see ourselves.

We may react behaviorally to infringements of our rights in a variety of ways. For example, we may seek to right the wrong by obtaining compensation or reparation. Even if we succeed in obtaining compensation, though, we may still feel resentment of the wrong. The degree to which we will experience these feelings will depend on our individual personality. There are some who allow resentment to loom large in their minds; others will give it less room, treating it as little more than a minor irritation. In spite of these differences in individual reactions, however, experiencing at least some degree of resentment toward wrongdoers appears to be a universal human phenomenon. In a sense, there is little point in delving further into the sources of resentment; what counts is that it is a feature of the way in which we interact with one another, and our human institutions must take this into account.

It is difficult to imagine a world in which feelings of resentment do not exist. Such a world would be a curiously flat place, distinctly lacking in contrast and emotion. It would be hard in such a world to determine what was right or wrong. If causing physical hurt to another, or defaming the person, for example, gave rise to no sense of resentment on the part of the injured person, then how could we tell whether or not it was wrong? Without feelings of resentment, everything would appear to be condoned, or tolerated, and therefore permissible, at least in a harm-based theory of morality. Resentment of wrong is intimately linked to our perception of right and wrong, and this perception enables us to recognize value in our relationships with the world about us. We need resentment, just as we need pleasure, to identify the good and its difference from the bad.[3]

Resentment may be absent in both those who are morally illiterate, who fail to see or understand the nature of wrongful conduct, and in those who are unduly tolerant. Those who are morally illiterate either have no notion of morality or, if they have such a notion, may see relatively few situations that involve their moral attention. This absence of resentment reveals a failure of moral cognition. Encouraging an appropriate level of resentment may be one way of promoting the development of moral sensitivity in this type of person.

Tolerance, a virtue respecting the autonomy of others, may lead to a diminution of resentment. Tolerance of the legitimate choices of others is desirable, but when tolerance is extended to wrongful acts, it undermines the whole nature of the moral enterprise. Encouraging the suppression of feelings of resentment may lead to tolerance of intolerable conduct. If it is resentment or anger that persuades us to condemn or act against cruelty or injustice, then these emotions must be given their proper room and not made to apologize for themselves in the face of overwhelming tolerance.[4]

Even if resentment is a necessary ingredient of a moral world, it does not follow that it must be given entirely free rein. A reflective morality—a morality that calls on us to consider our reasons for acting—requires of us two tasks in confronting resentment. The first is to identify the grounds on which the resentment has arisen.

This done, we must decide whether our resentment is justified. This inquiry goes both to the nature of the wrong itself—to ascertain whether an interest really has been infringed—and whether the wrongdoer is truly blameworthy. This latter question may reveal the presence of an excusing condition that makes resentment inappropriate. We do not blame those, for example, who are too young or mentally ill to be held accountable for their actions. It may be that there is initial resentment when such a person causes another harm, but this is quickly defused when the excuse is made known. There are no grounds for resenting what a very young child has done; the harm does not spring from deliberate malice. One might as well bear a grudge against the weather.

The second task is to keep our emotions from overwhelming us. Resentment has a destructive potential, both for the wronged person and for society, unless it is kept within bounds. For this reason, resentment should be limited in extent and, critically for our current theme, in duration. There are also considerations of just desert that point to a need to limit resentment; resentment should be proportional to the wrong we have suffered. Just as we disfigure ourselves psychologically by keeping alive our resentment over a minor wrong done 20 years ago, so too do we harm ourselves and others if we allow ourselves massive resentment over some trifling matter.

Limiting Resentment

We identified two grounds on which resentment should be controlled, one pragmatic and another moral. These will be considered in turn, to see how each might be applied in the case of the wrongs of the past.

Pragmatic Grounds

The pragmatic ground for drawing boundaries to our resentment of wrongs is based on the view that, were we not to do this, our life would become too cluttered. Our dealings with others are, in great measure, forward looking. It may be possible to live in the past—to view people and institutions in the light of values and standards that are no longer current or to make choices on the basis of information that is outdated—but such an approach is ultimately absurd. The rational person understands that we occupy the present, and that the shape of the present is dictated by how, in the past, we have planned for the future. Much of what we do, then, is directed toward securing our future. We save now for tomorrow, and make our investment calculations on the future behavior of the market; we study now to get a qualification that will stand us in good stead in several years' time. These decisions are forward-looking, even if in making them we draw on past experience to guide us.

In our relations with others, a sense of the past, present, and future also plays an important role. We are aware of the past conduct of those with whom we deal, but if we are wise, we do not allow the past to carry excessive weight in our decisions about the present and the future. For example, imagine that we are contemplating hiring an employee. The applicant's past is relevant in that it tells us what sort of person the applicant is, and it gives us grounds for deciding whether the person is capable of doing the job. The real question with which we are concerned, however, is not whether the applicant has been able to do a similar job in the past, but whether the person can do it in the future. So if we see that the applicant has had difficulties with the job in the past, we should not, on those grounds alone, decide that the person is incapable of doing it in the future. If we are being fair—which, of course, may require us to battle against prejudice—we should be prepared to discount an unsatisfactory past on the grounds that the applicant has changed.

The moral importance of this is reflected in laws that allow criminal convictions to be concealed or annulled after a certain period of time.[5] The philosophy of such legislation is that there comes a time at which a person may reasonably ask others to judge him or her for what he is now, rather than for what he or she was in the past. A conviction for theft 10 years ago tells us that, at that point, the convicted person acted dishonestly; a decade later it does not necessarily tell us that the person still acts dishonestly. Indeed, it could be argued that, if there is no evidence that the person has committed a criminal offense over a period of a decade, then that person has reformed. The cynic, of course, might suggest that what it means is that the person has simply avoided detection over that period, but such a view is objectionable both because it demands proof of a negative and because it represents a denial of just deserts. If we preclude the possibility of reform, then we effectively deny that moral effort deserves credit.

To limit the effect that the past should have on our decisions for the future is to acknowledge that the past will prevent us from making rational choices relating to that future. This is so because this past may no longer be relevant to the achievement of the future goal. In the employment example mentioned above, if we decide the appointment on the basis of the candidate's past performance rather than on the current and future ability, then we behave irrationally in relation to our objective of appointing the most competent applicant. We therefore make an irrational choice because our view is cluttered by the past.

Moral Grounds

Even if one is not persuaded by the pragmatic arguments in favor of limiting resentment, the moral grounds for doing so are compelling, and these operate both in respect of the magnitude of our resentment and its duration. There must be some correlation between the nature of the wrong and the magnitude of the response. This is a question of just deserts; a major wrong deserves a great deal of resentment, whereas a minor wrong deserves less. The explanation for why this should be so must be found in theories of punishment and in particular in the notion of retribution. If the moral balance is upset by the wrongdoing, then the measure of punishment required to rectify the imbalance must be appropriate.

The same notion is at work in relation to resentment. We are entitled to feel intense resentment over a serious wrong done to us. The hurt is intense because our loss is great, and therefore, the pain and the sense of wrong it produces will be correspondingly powerful. In the case of a minor wrong, though, there is no justification for feeling the degree of pain that would be produced by a major wrong. If we overreact, we do an injustice by attributing to the author of the pain responsibility for something that the act would normally not be expected to cause. This is a causally based objection. We should be held to account only for those events or states of affairs that our acts have produced and that we could reasonably be expected to foresee. To attribute greater responsibility is to lay at our door things that may be the fault of others—in this case the excessive resentment is the responsibility of the victim and of his or her failure to place things in proper perspective.

The same argument can be applied to the duration of resentment, where once again notions of just deserts appear to play a role. Ordinarily, resentment fades with the passage of time. This may be because of the consignment of the past to memory, and a consequent failure to recall, or it may be because we recognize the limited relevance of the past (the argument rehearsed above). The fact that resentment tends to disappear over time means that it should also be made to disappear over time, precisely because of the causation argument. Just as it is unacceptable to attribute an excessive level of hurt to one who could not have contemplated that such hurt should be caused by his action, so too is it wrong to attribute temporally distant hurt to one who could not have foreseen it. It would be unjust to reproach another for a minor wrong committed 5 years earlier. It is not foreseeable that hurt from a trivial wrong should extend for 5 years, and thus, the wrongdoer is not to blame for its persistence.

This discussion of resentment presupposes that reactive feelings will be allowed to run their normal course and that they are controlled by a sense of what is appropriate in terms of level and duration. Resentment, though, is susceptible to control by a further factor, forgiveness, which plays a crucial role in limiting the effect of the past on the present. Forgiveness is a concept of immense importance in our dealings with others. In one view forgiveness is a virtue that, if at all possible, we should cultivate. In another view, it is more than a virtue that we might choose to pursue; it is a moral duty. If such a duty exists, then the critical issue for our current theme is whether the passage of time accentuates this duty and requires us to forgive old wrongs, no matter how serious.

What Forgiveness Is

Joseph Butler, the 17th-century English theologian, saw forgiveness as a matter of overcoming the resentment caused by a wrongdoer.[6] This approach recognizes the consequences of resentment and prompts us to cast forgiveness as a means of forestalling revenge. Unless we forgive, we are likely to devote our energy to seeking revenge. Revenge is different from retribution in that it is claimed by the victim of the wrong—rather than by society—and it tends not to observe the strict rules of proportionality that apply when retribution is exacted.[7] A person who pursues revenge may seek to impose on the wrongdoer a greater level of pain than he himself suffered. In view of this, revenge is inherently anarchic; its unpredictability is socially unsettling, and its failure to observe bounds means that it creates new wrongs that will themselves prompt a response. Ultimately, revenge involves society in a spiral of long-lasting and destructive feuds.

Forgiveness, which is a deliberate act, is distinct from forgetting, which tends to be an involuntary process.[8] To forgive a person who has wronged us requires an effort, and it may be our moral duty to make that effort. To forget a wrong, by contrast, is something that usually, if not always, merely happens. We do not willingly let go of our resentment; it merely fades until it reaches the point at which it no longer has any effect on us. We get no moral credit for forgetting a wrong in contrast to forgiving a wrong—moral credit comes with effort to do the right thing, after all. Forgiveness is also to be distinguished from mercy. When mercy is shown, the wrong is not canceled; in fact, the resentment felt by the wronged person may be as strong as ever. To act mercifully is to mitigate the punishment that is exacted for the wrong, whether this is done because of a change in the attitude of the wrong-doer, or because the person who imposes punishment wishes to avoid further suffering or intends to set an example. Mercy says nothing about the relationship between the wrongdoer and the wronged; this relationship may never return to normal, as the relationship between the wrongdoer and the wronged may do after the decision to forgive is taken. Only when mercy has matured into forgiveness—or possibly when forgetfulness has taken over—can relations between the wrongdoer and the wronged recover that level of trust and good will that is required for ordinary human relations.

If forgiveness is forswearing resentment, why should it be a moral duty? We have previously suggested that there are pragmatic reasons why we should forgive. But is the moral duty to be founded on these pragmatic grounds alone, or is there something in the act of forgiving that makes it, from a deontological point of view, a morally worthy thing to do? This question takes us to the heart of our notion of human value and of our duty to treat others with the respect that their human condition deserves.

Let us assume that we owe to others a minimum duty of respect. This duty requires that we recognize the feelings of others as having some worth and significance. We should not, therefore, belittle others, even if we find their attitudes absurd, distasteful, or even evil. At all points, the dignity of the other must be acknowledged and observed, even if they have acted in such a way as to incur our justified resentment. This is the rationale for the belief that we should not subject others to cruel or unusual punishments, just as it is the rationale underpinning a whole raft of individual human rights, including the right to free speech.

If we recognize and value human dignity, then we must allow others the opportunity to assert their dignity. This means that they must be given the opportunity to act in a way that allows their moral essence to develop and be expressed. It is clearly wrong to prevent a child from pursuing moral development by inhibiting the growth of moral personality. Thus, to keep a child from finding out facts about the world is to stunt moral personality, wrongfully hindering the development of individual autonomy. These are special cases, of course, in that they involve situations in which we have power over others, as parents, teachers, or even jailers. The principle applies as easily in those cases where the leverage that we have over others is a concomitant of our normal social and moral dealings with them. In the ordinary course of such relationships, we engage with others as moral beings—we make claims on them, we recognize mutual obligations, and we make moral judgments as to how they (and we) behave toward one another.

Implicit in these day-to-day moral contacts is the notion that we will act with consistency and fairness, and this involves allowing others to achieve moral autonomy in their dealings with us. To pursue an analogy of moral conversation, one might then say that in engaging with others we should not prevent them from saying anything. To do so would be like visiting an art gallery with a friend and commenting on all the paintings while not allowing the friend to speak. Such an experience would be, for our friend, rather like trying to talk to the dentist when he questions you while working in your mouth—an inherently unequal relationship.

To refuse to forgive involves saying to the wrongdoer "What you have done determines what you, in my eyes, will always be. There is nothing you can do to change this." A failure to forgive "freezes" the wrongdoer in a particular moral posture and denies the person the chance to prove that he or she is anything but a morally worthless individual. It cripples his moral autonomy, and it asserts that he or she is a person of limited worth. In this respect, a lack of forgiving demeans the wrongdoer and offends the principle that there is always, in the least of people, some measure of residual human dignity. If we are to be serious in our recognition of human dignity and human rights, we have a moral duty to forgive.

It is also possible that a duty to forgive can be constructed on the foundations of our own duty of self-respect. Not to forgive is to prevent ourselves from developing our moral personality to its full extent. Forgiveness of others allows us to develop compassion, which is one of the salient features of the moral landscape. Without compassion in our lives, we are insensitive to a whole range of feeling and are morally smaller as a result. Of course, there is a major caveat to this: If we forgive too quickly, we can be seen to be demeaning ourselves by failing to show adequate self-respect. This is an issue of prime importance for our theme of old crimes, and we shall now turn to an analysis of it to see if it supports the proposition that past guilt should be kept alive, if not indefinitely, then at least for a substantial period of time. The somewhat troubling lesson here is that those who forgive too rapidly, although superficially admirable, are in fact in danger of weakening, rather than enhancing, the very human dignity that they would purport to cherish.

When to Forgive

On rare occasions we witness unconditional, immediate forgiveness of a serious wrong. This experience is arresting—we are accustomed to unforgiving attitudes and to the perpetuation of grievances; we are less familiar with rapid forgiveness. When it occurs, the forgiver is often held up as a moral example, as in the case of Cardinal Joseph Bernadin who, immediately after the termination of a civil claim against him, forgave a young man who had wrongly accused the cardinal of sexually molesting him as a child.[9] Perhaps even more striking is the example of those relatives of murder victims who actively campaign against the imposition of the death penalty and who profess their forgiveness of the perpetrators. One of the most moving accounts of this is to be found in the words of a mother whose daughter was abducted and killed while on a family camping trip. The mother describes how she eventually came to confront the murderer and ask the prosecutor not to seek the death penalty:

> Though I readily admit that I wanted to kill this man with my bare hands, by the time of the resolution of his crimes, I was convinced that my best and healthiest option was to forgive. In the twenty years since losing my daughter, I have been working with victims and their families and my experience has been consistently confirmed. Victim families have every right initially to the normal, valid, human response of rage, but those persons who retain a vindictive mind-set ultimately gives

the offender another victim. Embittered, tormented, enslaved by the past, their quality of life is diminished. However, unjustified, our unforgiveness undoes us.[10]

Are such people moral saints, whose example we should strive to follow, or is their reaction morally inappropriate? In answering this question, it is important to recognize that there is a proper time for forgiveness. To forgive prematurely may be as wrong as to forgive tardily.[11]

We have suggested that the act of forgiving is a communication to the wrongdoer that the wrong is no longer held against him. In a sense, this amounts to saying to the wrongdoer that resentment is no longer felt, but the process is more than an assurance that the wrong "no longer hurts"; it involves saying that the wrong "no longer matters." This statement touches on more than the personal feelings of the wronged person; it acknowledges the moral seriousness of the wrong itself. Rapid forgiveness implies that there is little to forgive, suggesting that the wrong has not created a significant moral affront. By contrast, the forgiveness that comes only after the passage of time emphasizes that the wrong is sufficiently substantial that its effect is felt for more than a few hours, days, or weeks.

The argument is sometimes made that forgiving the wrongdoer in no way diminishes the seriousness of the wrong. This view detaches a person's acts from the person himself. It is not as strange an idea as it may seem at first glance. This is the approach of the criminal law to the weighing of the tariffs of crimes, a process that focuses not on who the defendant is but on what was done.[12] A court may well condemn a criminal act in the strongest terms, and yet, in a case in which remorse has been shown or an effort has been made to reform, it may treat the offender with compassion. It is intelligible in this context to say that the act is abhorrent but the actor no longer is. If it is possible in this way to isolate the act from the actor, then forgiving the wrongdoer does not necessarily mean that the act itself has become acceptable.

This may be theoretically the case, but one may wonder whether this will work in practice. If wrongs are rapidly forgiven, the expressive function of punishment would rarely be served. There would surely be a danger that people might conclude that those acts that are rapidly forgiven are not really serious. They may reach this conclusion because they are familiar with their own reactive feelings and they link reactive feelings of resentment with moral wrongfulness. We know that an act is wrong because we know how we would feel if we were at the receiving end of that act. If we see others not feeling proper resentment, we may reach the conclusion that this is because what has been done to them is not really wrong.

It might be useful to add flesh to this last point by use of an example. In societies in which the racial oppression of Black people by White people was institutionalized and commonplace, many of the oppressors simply failed to see their conduct as wrong. This was because they believed that the subjugation of one race by another was part of the natural order. Indeed, in the worst modern example of such oppression, the apartheid state of South Africa, there was an elaborate ideology constructed to justify the permanent relegation of the majority population to an inferior status. This ideology was based on a bizarre mixture of Calvinist theology, meretricious history, and bogus anthropology.[13] It might have been expected that this ideology, and its concomitant practices of oppression, would fail rapidly, but it did not, and in its most virulent form, it effectively lasted for 4 decades following the victory of the Afrikaner-dominated National Party in 1948. To an extent, its longevity was a matter of sheer military and police might, but it survived also because the population was conditioned to accept the assumptions of the White supremacists. The oppressed in some cases accepted the presuppositions of their oppressors; for some time there was comparatively little outrage at what was done. The fact that many of the victims of apartheid did not protest vociferously contributed to the belief in the privileged White population that what was being done was simply not wrong. Acceptance of injustice can easily be read as suggesting that there is no injustice.

Making this point should not be interpreted as castigating the victims of injustice for allowing themselves to be oppressed. The difficulties of resisting tyranny may be too great for all but the heroes of a resistance movement, and the few of us who have not experienced tyranny can claim that we would not, ourselves, be passive in the face of evil. What the example does illustrate, though, is the proposition that reactive attitudes—anger, resentment, and the like—do play an important role in defining a wrong and in preventing the wrong from being understood as something normal or acceptable. Rapid forgiveness risks misrepresenting the true nature of the wrong. Anger is sometimes both righteous and necessary.

Becoming Party to the Wrong

One of the major arguments against premature forgiveness is that it implies complicity with the wrongdoer. This notion is a familiar one in the criminal law, in which accessorial criminal liability may attach not only to a person who plays an active part in the commission of a crime but also to one who fails to distance himself or herself sufficiently from the criminal act. In general, the criminal law is reluctant to impose liability for a failure to act, but in cases in which a person is drawn into a situation by virtue of a relationship with another or by position or status, there may be liability for failing to prevent an adverse consequence. For example, the senior police officer who fails to prevent a junior police officer from assaulting a suspect in the senior officer's presence might be considered an accessory to the crime of assault.

In cases of this nature, the criminal law justifies liability on the grounds that there is a specific duty to act. Unlike those cases in which liability for failure to act cannot be imposed because a general duty to act is simply too diffuse, obligations of this nature are clearly delineated. The failure to act is a failure of a particular person at a particular time. Failure to act makes one a party to the wrong because one had the duty to prevent the wrong, had the power to do so, and nonetheless decided not to act. Such a failure can be said to have played a causal role in the eventual outcome. For example, that Alan does nothing to stop Beth from producing some consequence justifies the conclusion that Alan is causally responsible, or at least shares the causal responsibility, for its occurrence.

How far does this analogy apply to the act of forgiving? The person who forgives the act of another plays no causal role in the event: The act has already taken place, and the person is not in a position to stop it. In that respect at least the person's position differs from the position of one who is treated as an accomplice by virtue of a failure to act. There is, however, another sense in which premature forgiveness may be said to play a similar causal role, in that it has an effect on future acts of the same kind. If we prematurely forgive another for a wrongful act, then it is reasonable to think that we might be encouraging that person to do a similar thing in the future or, alternatively, by forgiving, we might be encouraging another in the belief that that person's own future wrongful acts of the same type will be similarly forgiven. Forgiveness then becomes a social act, which bears not only on those wrongs with which it is immediately concerned but also on all future wrongs. It is an act, then, that defines a moral stance toward conduct of a particular sort and that indicates how the person exercising forgiveness and other similarly situated people may be expected to respond to future examples of such conduct.

These grounds for controlling forgiveness are perhaps best illustrated in the example of war crimes. The practice of prosecuting war crimes is not only inspired by the notions of retribution; there also is at work in such cases a clear desire on the part of the prosecutors to make it known to those who commit war crimes that they will never get away with it. The prosecution of war crimes therefore seeks to underline the fact that, although circumstances of conflict may allow crimes to be committed with impunity, there will be a day of reckoning. These prosecutions have always been strongly influenced by a desire to encourage others in different conflicts to take note of the fact that they, too, are accountable for what they do. As forcefully argued by those who oppose impunity in the case of human rights violations, forgiveness of war crimes may weaken the international community's message that the murder of civilians or crimes against humanity will not be tolerated.[14] Against this background, the natural human inclination to forgive must be held in check.

The same argument might be made of the prosecution of other wrongs. Child sexual abuse is a substantial wrong capable of marring the life of the victim. Again there may be a deterrent argument against forgiveness if the result of this would be to encourage others in the belief that they have a chance of avoiding punishment and blame simply by requesting forgiveness after a period of time.

This cautious view of forgiveness is not universally accepted. There is a view that forgiving in fact sends out no message of condonation and that to forgive is a sign of moral strength, rather than an inclination to condone wrongdoing. This point is made by Cheshire Calhoun, who questioned the prominent role accorded to resentment:

> In social contexts where "everyone knows" what the wrong acts and who the moral equals are, and where wrongdoing frequently though not invariably meets with protests or penalties, the average person would not likely interpret failure to protest as condonation. If I catch a neighborhood adolescent bashing my mailbox and forgive him, he might think me exceptionally nice or wimpish. He surely would not infer that bashing mailboxes is morally permissible, or will not be penalized, or that I am his moral equal. Nor do I necessarily worsen his behavior, since by forgiving him, he may come to see that he is harming real people, people he might like. As a point about human moral psychology, the idea that resentment, protest and punishment best effect moral improvement is surely misguided. The last thing some need is yet more resentment and punishment.[15]

Even if punishment does little to improve people, there are other interests at stake here. We are concerned not just that the offender get his just deserts but also with the effect of our response on society as a whole. To forgive a single offender does not necessarily imply to people in general that the conduct in question is right, but if all offenders were to be forgiven, or even if a substantial number were to be forgiven for a particular wrong, then surely the community's sense that the action in question was wrong would be weakened. This would appear to be the philosophy of zero-tolerance policing, which proceeds on the basis that the condonation of minor criminal acts is directly connected to a boldness in relation to more major crimes.[16] Whether these policies are solely responsible for falling crime rates is a matter of debate; they have, nonetheless, been taken by some as vindicating the notion that an unambiguous message is effective: Wrongdoing will not be tolerated, or readily forgiven. Without this message, the temptation is to assume acceptance of the conduct in question. So Calhoun could be wrong: The adolescent who vandalizes her mailbox is likely to assume that his conduct is not wrong, as are his companions who observe the impunity with which he acts. If no one resents gratuitous damage to their property, except passingly, then we can be sure that it will in the future be considerably more difficult to assert that damage to property merits opprobrium and punishment.

Conditions of Forgiveness

There are two sorts of forgiveness: unconditional and conditional. Unconditional forgiveness may be offered with or without the request of the wrongdoer, and it implies the cancellation of resentment, whether the wrongdoer does anything further in relation to the wronged party. It is possible to forgive a wrongdoer unilaterally, even if he has done nothing to indicate that he has changed his attitude toward what he did. In such circumstances, there is no question of forgiveness being dependent on repentance. Indeed, forgiveness of this sort could be extended to the entirely unapologetic wrongdoer who persists either in denying that wrong was done or who even shows that he or she does not care about the harm that he or she has caused. The most notorious example of a failure to atone, and its flaunting, was provided by the war criminal Klaus Barbie. Barbie, whose acts of callous torture in Nazi-occupied Lyons were eventually exposed in a long-delayed trial, was confronted in court by one of his victims who had been in her teens when she was subjected to torture.[17] In spite of the harrowing evidence of what had happened, and her dignified account of her suffering, Barbie showed himself to be completely unmoved, remarking that his only regret was that he had not finished her off at the time.

In the face of such quintessential evil, who would feel inclined to forgive Barbie? His attitude puts his case into a quite different category from many others who, in similar circumstances to his, participated in the atrocities of the Nazi war years. Many attempted to change their identity and vanish; others, when apprehended and identified, sought to transfer blame or simply to deny responsibility for what happened. Some showed regret and repentance and accepted punishment. All of these reactions seem unsurprising; what confounds the imagination is Barbie's continued attachment, so long after the event, to these acts of cruelty. Barbie, it would seem to many, had not the slightest claim to forgiveness.

His case is, of course, an extreme example. There are other instances of reluctance to apologize that make much the same point. There is no comparison between the moral quality of Klaus Barbie and Richard Nixon, whatever might be felt about the apparent flaws in the latter's character. What justifies the introduction of Nixon into this company is his curious refusal to apologize following the disclosure of wrongdoing in the Watergate burglary and its aftermath. Nixon never apologized for this, even when he was faced with irrefutable evidence of the gross betrayal of the trust that had been placed in him by the electorate. In his resignation speech to the nation, he said

> I regret deeply any injuries that may have been done in the course of events that led to this decision. I would say only that if some of my judgments were wrong, and some were wrong, they were made in what I believed at the time to be the in the best interest of the Nation.[18]

As Nicholas Tavuchis pointed out, this was not an apology and was never taken to be one by Nixon or the public, even if it was the closest the former president came to saying that he was sorry.[19] Had he apologized, the nation's verdict on this aspect of his presidency might have been more charitable, as was suggested by editorial comment at the time: "It would have been easier for the nation to stress his accomplishments," observed the *New York Times,* "if he himself had shown more candor about his shortcomings."[20]

A failure to repent, then, makes forgiveness more difficult, if not impossible. Repentance is a way of "divorcing oneself" from the wrongdoing; the person who repents, then, acknowledges that his or her act was wrong and indicates that he or she does not wish to be associated with it. Insofar as the original act was interpreted by its victim—and others—as implying the victim's lack of worth, the act of repentance cancels this statement. The relationship between the parties is therefore changed. The wrongdoer no longer claims that his or her interests count for more than those of the wronged person, and this restores moral equality.

Such a view fits well with a retributive view of punishment. Punishment itself does not require that there be repentance, but the notion of moral balance that occupies a central place in retributive theories is sensitive to repentance. The suffering of the punished wrongdoer appears to restore the moral equilibrium. According to retributive theory, repentance is, in a sense, a form of suffering in that it also involves pain. In acknowledging the wrongdoing, the wrongdoer expresses regret—the contemplation of these acts should cause him pain. There is humiliation too: Punishment humiliates the wrongdoer by taking from him or her the equivalent of that which he or she has wrongfully taken from another. In a similar way repentance involves humiliation, although in this case the humiliation is one that the penitent imposes on himself or herself.

Apology plays an important role in the restoration of social order. Excuses and justifications detach the actor from the full implications of the act. Apology does not do this; the person who apologizes recognizes the wrong that he or she has done and asks for forgiveness. This recognition, and this request, are both necessary for society's norms to survive the infringement and if, crucially, the social institutions that enable people to live in harmony are to be repaired. In this analysis, the wrongdoer who indicates through an apology that he or she repents of his wrongdoing conveys the message that he or she can be trusted in the future and that he or she wishes to have normal social relations with those that he or she has wronged.

The importance of smoothing the course of our social relations has led to the institutionalization of ways to express regret and to ask for forgiveness. The shape that apology takes varies from society to society. In circumstances in which emotional candor is particularly highly rated, what will count will be the perceived sincerity of the apology. In other circumstances, there may be greater emphasis on a particular ritual of apology, the important matter here being that the expected form is observed. Where form counts, the public significance of apology is likely to be stressed. The fact that the wrongdoer has made the appropriate gesture indicates to all that the humiliation of the victim is rectified. Social order, which relies on conventions and expectations of their observance, is strengthened by the act of apology.

We have seen that repentance makes it easier to forgive, but is it an absolute prerequisite of forgiveness? Again the problem is that of endorsement of the act. If we forgive the unrepentant wrongdoer, then we run the same risk as is run by the person who gives premature forgiveness: No message is given as to the wrongfulness of the act. For this reason, it may be reasonable to require repentance—or possibly punishment—before forgiveness is forthcoming, provided, of course, that the original wrong is sufficiently weighty to require repentance. Some wrongs will be so minor that the wrongdoer's failure to repent will not destabilize any norms. An act of minor selfishness or thoughtlessness may require no apology for normal relations to continue; a serious act of violence or theft may be so disruptive of trust that without repentance forgiveness is unwise.

Applying Our Observations

By now, we have established enough about forgiveness to test our view against a selection of cases. We have seen that there is a duty to forgive based both on pragmatic grounds (nursed resentments clutter our lives in society) and on moral grounds (refusing to forgive another denies that person the dignity that is deserved). We have also seen that forgiveness should not be too rapid, lest it undermine the moral condemnation of the wrong, and it may require some form of apology on the part of the wrongdoer. Now let us apply these observations to cases of the sort that we discussed in chapter 1.

As one might expect, minor wrongs are the easiest to forgive, but this does not prevent their sometimes being instructive. During the World War II, an American serviceman stationed in England stole a bicycle in a quiet country village. History moved on; the war in Europe came to an end, and he returned to the United States. But he retained the memory of what he had done, and 40 years later, pricked by conscience, he worked out the value of the bicycle, established what that sum would have become had it been invested and attracted compound interest, and then, in a magnificent gesture, gave that money to the village. His action was widely reported in the press and attracted very favorable comments.[21] Should he be forgiven?

Of course. Forgiveness had been handsomely earned in this case because of the gesture that he had made to set right the scales. But what if he had not made any gesture of this sort? We suspect that we would probably still be inclined to forgive him because of two factors: the relative smallness of the crime and the length of time that had passed. Not to forgive him in such circumstances would be to manifest precisely that attitude of retentiveness that we described as "cluttering." Notions of proportionality also play a part in this sort of assessment. The loss of a bicycle is not invariably a small thing, but it is not a matter on which one would ordinarily ponder for years. Even if he had never returned it, this is not a matter that most people would be inclined to bother about after 40 years. This suggests that to mention the trivial wrongs of the past is almost mischievous—it threatens to disturb the tranquility of our relations with one another.

Matters become quite different when we turn to substantial wrongs. A rapist, for example, may find his victim unwilling to forgive him, even if the rape took place 15 or 20 years before. Why is this? Surely it is because what has been done has such an effect on the victim's life that the hurt is still present. In this sort of case, the wrong does not belong to the past because its effect is still being felt. The stolen bicycle is likely to be forgotten—it has no effect on the present—the rapist's victim, however, may be permanently harmed. Forgiveness in such cases may be much more difficult, and indeed it may be something that we cannot realistically expect of the victim, just as we might not be able to expect it of the victims of Rudolf Kos, the sexually abusive priest discussed in chapter 1. His victims understandably feel that their lives have been ruined by what Kos did to them. Their image of themselves as men, their sense of their sexual identity, was shattered by their experiences, and some of them feel that these will never be restored. They may be wrong in this— they may ultimately recover—but there do seem to be many victims of this sort who feel that recovery is beyond them.

How much more difficult still must forgiveness be in a case in which the crime is one of murder. It is probably true to say that the vast majority of those who survived the great mass murder campaigns of the 20th century, those caught up in the Holocaust in Europe or the millions of families who suffered Communist slaughters in China or Cambodia, do not forgive those who were responsible for their suffering. And this is entirely understandable. Would we say, though, that they have a duty to forgive the Nazis, the Red Guards, or the Khmer Rouge? In the first place, such a suggestion coming from any one who had not actually been the victim of such outrages would probably be refuted on the grounds that forgiveness is personal and that it is only those who suffer who can forgive.[22] There are objections, however, that lie beyond this. Some wrongs, perhaps, are so great that the usual factors in favor of forgiveness are outweighed by the immensity of the injury sustained. For example, the argument that old wrongs clutter the present does not apply. These wrongs are so weighty that they justifiably loom large in the minds of those who have suffered them. Then again, there is the question of repentance. Germany has indeed shown repentance for the wrongs committed by the Nazis, but it is not modern Germany as a state that is being blamed for what happened. The moral responsibility for what happened rests with those who actually perpetrated the wrong or who, through culpable inaction and turning a blind eye, became party to the wrong. If repentance is a necessary precondition for forgiveness, the Nazis themselves can never be forgiven, at the least, because they did not repent.

It is entirely understandable that those concerned with bringing justice to World War II criminals should take the position that their task will not be done until the last of those who were guilty of these crimes have answered for them. This means that trials such as that of Papon, the French collaborator who participated in the dispatch of death convoys from Vichy, France, will continue, even if Papon stood trial at age 87.[23] As usually happens, such people assert their innocence, which hardly encourages sympathy for them. Would we feel differently toward a man in his late 80s who stood in the dock and said "I am guilty. I regret what I did, and I seek forgiveness"? Or would we insist on his punishment? On balance, we feel that when a wrong is so great, forgiveness cedes to the need for the law to declare the wrong, and this can only be done by punishment.

There is also the question of keeping faith with the victims. The dead are still part of the human community in one sense; we feel links with them, and their presence is not forgotten. In a curious sense, we see the dead as having certain rights, and there may be cases in which these rights must be vigorously asserted by the living. As time passes, though, the memory of the dead fades, and their role in the living human community weakens. At that point, the imperative of forgiveness may reassert itself, and letting go of the past not only is wise but becomes the right thing to do.

Endnotes

1. Frans de Waal, *Chimpanzee politics: Power and sex among apes* (Baltimore: John Hopkins University Press, 1998) at 27.
2. See Aurel Kolnai, "Forgiveness," *Proceedings of the Aristotelean Society* 74 (1973–1974):91–106; Jeffrie Murphy and Jean Hampton, *Forgiveness and mercy* (Cambridge, England: Cambridge University Press, 1988) at 79. For a discussion of the role of emotions in forgiveness, see Robert Roberts, "Forgiveness," *American Philosophical Quarterly,* 32 (1995):289–303.
3. For a view that accords resentment a central role in moral theory, see Peter Strawson, "Freedom and resentment." In *Studies in the philosophy of thought and action*, Peter Strawson, Ed. (Oxford, England: Oxford University Press, 1968) at 71.
4. For a convincing attack on misplaced tolerance, see Tara Smith, "Tolerance and forgiveness: Virtues or vices?" *Journal of Applied Philosophy* 14 (1997):31–41.
5. See Richard Nygaard, "On the role of forgiveness in criminal sentencing," *Seton Hall Law Review,* 27 (1997):980–1022.
6. Joseph Butler, *Fifteen sermons* (London: Bell, 1949).
7. See discussion in Susan Jacoby, *Wild justice: The evolution of revenge* (London: Collins, 1985).
8. Most writers on forgiveness see it as a choice: Forgiving is an act that it is *done* by the actor in the same way as he writes a letter or signs a contract. Robin Downie, "Forgiveness," *Philosophical Quarterly* 15 (1965):128–134; and Joanna North, "Wrongdoing and forgiveness," *Philosophy* 62 (1987):499–508. For an alternative view, which stresses the importance of the disposition to forgive, see David Novitz, "Forgiveness and self-respect," *Philosophy and Phenomenological Research* 58 (1998):299–315.
9. C. McCarthy, "The bishops don't have a prayer," *The Washington Post,* Nov. 20, 1993, Saturday, final ed., at A23.
10. Marietta Jaeger, "The power and reality of forgiveness: Forgiving the murderer of one's child." In *Exploring forgiveness,* Robert Enright and Joanna North, Eds. (Madison: University of Wisconsin Press, 1998) at 9–14.
11. Premature forgiveness may mean that the wronged person lacks self-respect. For a discussion of this aspect of forgiveness, see Margaret Holmgren, "Forgiveness and the intrinsic value of persons," *American Philosophical Quarterly* 30 (1993):341–352.
12. Andrew von Hirsch, *Past or future crime* (Manchester, England: Manchester University Press, 1986) at 19–28.
13. Tracy Kuperus, *State, civil society, and apartheid in South Africa: An examination of the Dutch-Reformed Church–state relations* (New York: St. Martin's Press, 1999).
14. *Campaign against impunity: Portrait and plan of action* (Montreal, Quebec, Canada: International Centre for Human Rights and Democratic Development, 1997).

15. Cheshire Calhoun, "Changing one's heart," *Ethics* 103 (1992):76–96.
16. Katherine Beckett, *Making crime pay: Law and order in contemporary American politics* (New York: Oxford University Press, 1997).
17. Alain Finkiekraut, *Remembering in vain: The Klaus Barbie trial and crimes against humanity* (New York: Columbia University Press, 1992).
18. Theodore White, *Breach of faith: The fall of Richard Nixon* (New York: Atheneum, 1975) at 343.
19. Nicholas Tavuchis, *Mea culpa: A sociology of apology and reconciliation* (Stanford, CA: Stanford University Press, 1991) at 55.
20. Anthony Lewise, "Editorial," *The New York Times,* Aug. 10, 1974, at 29.
21. "Ex-GI repays bicycle debt 100-fold," *The Reuter Library Report,* May 10, 1992, Sunday, BC cycle.
22. Simon Wiesenthal, *The sunflower: On the possibilities and limits of forgiveness* (New York: Schoken Books, 1997).
23. Arno Klarsfeld, *Papon: Un verdict Français* [Papon: The French verdict] (Paris, France: Ramsay, 1998). See also Bertram Gordon, "Collaboration, retribution, and crimes against humanity: The Touvier, Bousquet, and Papon affairs," *Contemporary French Civilization* 19 (1995): 250.

Chapter 4
WHEN TIME MATTERS MOST:
Statutes of Limitations

Most crimes are not prosecuted.[1] The simplest explanation for this is the failure to report crimes; offenses that are not reported to the authorities cannot be prosecuted. Serious problems result from the nonreporting of all crimes; sexual offenses, however, present problems common to the prosecution of all old crimes and many unique challenges for the criminal justice system that test the structure of the law of limitations. Thus, we explore limitations in the context of sexual offense as one of the central themes of this chapter.

A high proportion of serious sexual crimes are never the subject of complaint, whether through shame or fear or because the victim wishes to avoid the conflict and ruptured relations that may follow criminal proceedings. It is difficult to be precise about the incidence of these crimes because they are ordinarily committed in private and, therefore, may lack objective proof that a crime occurred. In any study dealing with the frequency of nonreporting, therefore, there is a lingering question about verification of the actual number of crimes committed. One Canadian report on the subject concluded that in the case of young male victims of sexual offenses, 9 out of 10 keep the incident a closely guarded secret, whereas the comparable calculation for female victims is 3 out of 4.[2] Another study of victims of childhood incest reported that only 3 of the 40 participants in the study brought the matter to the attention of the police.[3] Numerous studies confirm a high incidence of nonreporting in the case of sexual assaults in general on children, with the rates of nonreporting being estimated between 50% and 90%.[4] This broad range of figures highlights the inherent difficulty of the topic of sexual abuse: Many of the features of the problem are contested, uncertain, or ambiguous, and there are widely differing views as to the importance that should be given to the problem. Just as there are those who argue that society has conspired to conceal the extent of the problem, thereby effectively condoning the continued sexual exploitation of vulnerable people, there are those who take the view that excessive interest will result in false accusations and injustice.[5]

In some cases, the reasons that may deter reporting these crimes may also operate to delay reporting. If this happens, the victim may conclude that his or her criminal complaint has fallen on deaf ears. Most legal systems recognize statutes of limitations that describe the time period within which a prosecution must be brought or abandoned. These rules operate without regard to the persuasiveness of the proof available in an individual case or the magnitude of the crime. Thus, any discussion of the prosecution of old crimes must come to terms with the way in which statutes of limitations operate. Statutes of limitations have drawn considerable criticism from those who feel that they undeservedly give greater weight to the interests of defendants than to those of victims.

In this chapter, we focus on the application of statutes of limitations to the prosecution of old crimes. Our analysis takes us through a consideration of the limitation rules that apply to all major crimes and in particular to war crimes and crimes against humanity and then narrows to the unique problems of delayed prosecution of child sexual abuse. Finally, we consider the choices that society faces in choosing between any fixed period of limitations, which arbitrarily permits some cases to escape punishment, and the absence of one.

A Brief History of the Statute of Limitations

Under U.S. Law

The rule that the state may not pursue a criminal wrong after the lapse of some time is not a feature of all legal systems. Indeed, the rule was not widely accepted in the English common law.[6] However, in the Roman law-based jurisdictions of continental Europe and Latin America, the state has always accepted time limits for bringing prosecutions. In the United States, in spite of the English common law background of American law, the principle of limitation was accepted at a very early stage and has been applied ever since.[7] A general limitation period of 1 year on the prosecution of crimes applied in colonial Massachusetts as early as 1652, and similar statutes were introduced in other states during the 18th century. Federal crimes have been subject to a limitation period since 1790.

The reason why limitation periods were introduced is not clear. One possible explanation is that it was an example of the influence of Roman legal theory that was, to some legal thinkers of the early United States, more ideologically attractive than English common law. It is easy to imagine how a revolutionary society eager to overthrow a discredited political system might be attracted by the notion of the fresh start implicit in the concept of limitation. For whatever reason, statutes of limitation are now applied in the vast majority of states, with only Wyoming[8] having no limitations and a handful of states lacking limitations for the prosecution of felonies.

The precise periods chosen for limitation law vary. In the United States, homicide—both murder and manslaughter—are almost invariably exempted from the application of statutes of limitations and can be prosecuted at any time. For crimes other than homicide, it is usual to find a distinction made between felonies and misdemeanors, with a longer limitation period applied to felonies. The Texas provisions are fairly typical. Under the terms of the Texas Code of Criminal Procedure, more serious felonies, including certain thefts involving breach of trust, cannot be prosecuted after 10 years, whereas a period of 5 years applies for other felonies and a 3-year period for misdemeanors.[9] The decision to categorize offenses for these purposes turns on the legislature's perception of the gravity of the offense and the difficulties inherent in bringing prosecution. Thus, for example, the Texas Legislature recently amended the statute of limitations for aggravated sexual assault to include it in the 10-year period for serious felonies.[10] In addition, the Legislature has chosen to treat offenses committed on children as a special case. Not only is there a 10-year limitation period for these crimes, but this period does not begin to run until the victim reaches his or her 18th birthday.

Under International Law

The issue of limitations has also proved to be important in relation to international crimes, particularly war crimes or crimes against humanity, that is, murder, enslavement, starvation, or deportation against citizens on racial, religious, political, or national grounds. International criminal law is a relatively new phenomenon, which has attracted considerable attention following the creation of an international court of criminal justice based in the Netherlands under the auspices of the United Nations. The scope of this system of international criminal justice is limited to crimes against humanity and war crimes, but it represents a significant step in a development that, with respect to war crimes, can be traced back at least several centuries. The idea that there are certain humanitarian standards to be expected in the conduct of war found expression in a number of codes and articles of war, with some, like the Articles of War of the Free Netherlands, dating back to the late 16th century.[11]

In the 20th century, particularly after World War I, a growing tendency emerged to identify certain acts as "crimes against humanity" that could be tried by any state that found itself in a position to do so, even if the crime had not been committed on its territory. This represented a major departure from the previous willingness of states to concern themselves only with acts performed within their immediate territorial jurisdiction. World War II brought a renewed determination to prosecute war crimes, and even before the end of the conflict, the Allies issued the Declaration of Moscow of 1943, stating their intention to punish war crimes after the cessation of hostilities. The Nuremberg and Tokyo trials of major war criminals were a direct result of this declaration, and these trials firmly established in the international consciousness that crimes of this nature would be punished under international law.[12]

Alongside this assertion of international jurisdiction, there was also a national practice of punishing war criminals under domestic legal systems, some of which had embodied international treaties on the subject, such as the Geneva Convention, into their national law. Many of these trials took place many years after the commission of the crimes in question. Both Germany and Austria, for example, whose nationals were prominent perpetrators of some of the most serious war crimes of the 20th century, continued to commence trials into the final decade of the 20th century, as did France. By 1988, the Federal Republic of Germany, which accepted responsibility for the crimes of the Nazi era, had tried over 91,000 people for war crimes,[13] and even if many war criminals from that era escaped punishment in one way or another—including flight abroad—the federal government continued to pursue offenders without any concession to limitations. Although German criminal law, like most continental European systems, has limitation periods even for serious offenses, it was amended to ensure that these did not apply in any case involving either genocide or murder under, respectively, Articles 220 and 211 of the Penal Code. This meant that prosecutions of World War II criminals were able to continue into the 1990s and, theoretically, could even continue into the 21st century. In 1991, for instance, Germany extradited and tried Josef Schwammberger, the Nazi commander of a Jewish ghetto and slave labor camp in Poland, who had sought refuge in Argentina, convicting him of murder and sentencing him to life imprisonment.[14] Austria also acted to exclude limitations in such crimes, introducing a law in 1965 that precludes the operation of limitation periods in the case of war crimes and crimes against humanity.[15]

The French experience has been mixed, in large part because of the difficulty that the country experienced in coming to terms with its collaborationist past. There were, however, a number of war crime trials in France more than 40 years after the country's liberation. The most prominent of these was the trial of Klaus Barbie, who had headed the Gestapo in Lyons and who had fled to a clandestine existence in South America. Barbie was expelled from Bolivia in 1983 and taken to France, where he was accused of over 340 crimes, including a number of crimes against humanity. He was convicted in 1987 and sentenced to life imprisonment.[16]

Barbie's trial raised important issues of limitations. Under French law, crimes of war are subject to limitations provisions, and these, it appeared, would operate to bar Barbie's prosecution for offenses under the French Penal Code. The prosecution argued, however, that he was charged with crimes against humanity, which were not subject to any period of limitation, and that on these grounds he could still be convicted. This argument was accepted by the *Cour de Cassation*, France's highest court of appeal, which acknowledged that the principles of international criminal law had been embodied in French domestic law.[17] This principle was responsible, too, for the eventual conviction in 1994 of Paul Touvier, a French collaborator, who had escaped justice for a considerable time after being given sanctuary by some elements within the Catholic Church. His earlier acquittal on the grounds of inadequate evidence had been heavily criticized, and it was only after reversal by the *Cour de Cassation* that he was eventually convicted for a single incident.[18]

Tardy war crime prosecutions were also undertaken in Australia, where a number of people suspected of participating in atrocities during World War II had emigrated after 1945. Australia, like the United Kingdom and Canada, has no statute of limitations in criminal matters. After the publication of a government report that concluded that a substantial number of unpunished war criminals were living in the country, the Attorney General announced in Parliament that the government was convinced that "justice must be done, no matter how much time has passed since the events in question."[19] This statement was followed by the creation of a task force charged with investigating these cases and presenting evidence to prosecutors. A number of trials ensued, but these were markedly unsuccessful from the prosecution point of view, largely because of the difficulty of obtaining reliable evidence after the passage of so many years but also because of problems associated with prosecuting older defendants. In two of the trials, the ill health of the defendant materially affected proceedings, leading to the abandonment of one trial—that of Heinrich Wagner—after the accused had a heart attack.[20]

The issue of delay was raised in one of these Australian prosecutions, *D. P. P. v. Polyukhovich*.[21] The 72-year-old defendant in this case was charged with the murder of a number of civilians in the Ukraine between 1941 and 1943. His defense relied on a number of arguments, including the proposition that a 51-year delay in prosecution was grounds for nonprosecution. This issue was directly addressed by the Supreme Court of South Australia, which acknowledged that such a delay was "enormously long" and "of unprecedented length" but concluded that in such a case the court should balance the interests involved to reach a conclusion on whether the delay was unfair to the defendant. In this case, the court did not conclude that the delay made a fair trial impossible. The trial, however, eventually did not proceed because of inadequate evidence.

In international criminal law, as the *Cour de Cassation* recognized in the Barbie trial, there has been strong support for rejecting any limitation period. The issue is not specifically mentioned, however, in the Geneva Conventions, first opened for signature by the International Red Cross in 1949, which deal with the treatment of prisoners, nor is it included in the Genocide Convention of the United Nations of 1948. Yet in the period after World War II, international law scholars frequently expressed the view that there should be no limitation period for war crimes and crimes against humanity.[22] This support was translated, to an extent, into concrete terms with the drafting of two international instruments specifically intended to exclude limitations in these circumstances. These were the United Nations' 1968 *Convention on the Non-Applicability of Statutory Limitations to Crimes Against Humanity and War Crimes*[23] and a more regional treaty, the Council of Europe's 1974 identically named convention.[24] The effect of these conventions, however, has been marginal; they have been ratified by very few states. Consequently, their effect in creating a rule of customary international law is diminished, even if they represent what is today probably the clear consensus on the matter.

When the Statute Begins to Run

In the normal course of events, the limitation period begins to run when the act that may be the subject of prosecution occurs. So, for example, in the case of a bank robbery in a state that recognizes a 10-year statute of limitations for such crimes, a prosecution brought 10 years and one day after the date of the bank robbery is subject to dismissal on limitations grounds. Not all cases are so clear.

Prosecution is not necessarily ruled out merely because the limitation period appears to have run its course. As always, there are exceptions to the rule. If the perpetrator is "in flight from justice," then the statute is tolled (that is, it does not run) during that period. This covers not only those situations in which an offender leaves the country to escape detection or apprehension, but also those situations in which the offender merely changes residences or attempts to change identity to avoid prosecution. To claim the protection of the statute of limitations, offenders must live openly and take no steps to conceal their crimes. This last requirement has proved problematic in the case of crimes, such as embezzlement, which are by their very nature concealed. In such a case, it may be impossible for the crime to be detected until the perpetrator leaves his or her post. Accordingly, there are both statutory provisions and court decisions that suspend the commencement of the limitation period until the point at which the crime could reasonably have been detected.

There are also exceptions that toll the running of the statute of limitations in the case of "continuing crimes," crimes that do not consist of a single act but that are made up of either a series of acts or of a state of affairs that persists over a period, such as conspiracy. A criminal conspiracy requires that the parties reach an agreement to pursue a criminal purpose, which initiates the conspiracy. The conspiracy continues in existence until the objective is reached or it is abandoned. In general, the statute of limitations begins to run only when the conspirators no longer share their common purpose, which may be an appreciable time after the making of the initial agreement. In the case of a conspiracy to rob a bank, if one of the conspirators engages in money laundering to hide the proceeds 1 year after the robbery itself, the statute of limitations on the conspiracy charge—for all of the bank robbery conspirators—begins to run from the time of the money laundering, not from the date of the robbery. By contrast, sexual abuse may not be treated as a continuing crime, even if it persists over a considerable period. Courts generally treat each act of abuse as a separate offense, with the result that the limitation period runs from the date of each act.

Another exception provides that the statute of limitations does not run while the perpetrator conceals the crime. If an embezzler, for example, conceals the fact that money is missing from the accounts, the statute of limitations will not run until the discrepancy has been discovered. For obvious reasons, it is harder to conceal offenses against the person (e.g., assault), and for this reason some courts have taken the view that these crimes, by their very nature, cannot be concealed.[25] Other courts, however, have been prepared to find concealment in cases of sexual abuse, and this has enabled the prosecution to bring charges beyond the limitation period. An example of this approach is *Crider v. State*[26] in which a father was convicted of sexually abusing his two daughters in respect of acts committed more than 5 years before prosecution was instituted. The defendant argued that the applicable 5-year period of limitation excluded these particular acts, but the court found that he had threatened his daughters and that these threats amounted to concealment. By contrast, in other cases where the perpetrator has allegedly threatened the victim if the offense is revealed, courts have declined to find concealment because the allegations have not satisfied the high threshold imposed for the application of this exception to the normal running of the statute of limitations.[27]

Other courts have tolled the statute of limitations absent specific threats. In *Danielski v. State,*[28] for example, the Minnesota Supreme Court found that the continuation of parental power over the victim was sufficient to toll the statute of limitations. The court's reasoning was not that this control amounted to concealment, but that it was grounds for holding that it was a continuing offense. The abuse of parental authority was an essential feature of the crime charged, and the court found that this abuse continued until the age of majority.

Fair Trials and Memory

Barring a criminal prosecution because of the statute of limitations may strike those affected by the crime as a perverse legal technicality. If there is persuasive evidence of the commission of the crime and the perpetrator, then why should there be no prosecution? There are cogent arguments in favor of limitations that are distinct from the issues of forgiveness discussed in chapter 3. The most powerful of these other arguments is that bringing a late prosecution deprives the defendant of the right to a fair trial. This is not to suggest that the neutrality of the court is compromised by the delay in prosecution; it suggests rather that the defendant is unable to marshal the relevant evidence against charges relating to events so far in the past. In chapter 6, we discuss limits on the reliability of human memory and our capacity to recall past events accurately. Although some aspects of the workings of human memory are not fully understood or are contested, there is wide agreement that the effect of time on memory is, on the whole, deleterious.[29] It is therefore safe to assume that our own recollection of what we did 10 years ago, and the recollection of witnesses to our conduct, will be less reliable than the equivalent recollections of what we did

1 week ago. For this reason, it will be more difficult for us to defend ourselves against charges relating to 10-year-old events than 1-week-old events.

The ability to defend oneself against a criminal charge is an essential requirement of American criminal procedure. A critical component of this ability is the recollection of relevant events.[30] If the defendant's memory of an offense and the events surrounding it has disappeared, then the ability to offer testimony, to identify other potential witnesses, and to assist in preparing cross-examination of prosecution witnesses is seriously compromised.

Courts reach varying and sometimes inconsistent results when they attempt to ascertain whether the defendant's memory problems should abate prosecution. Although amnesia has an obvious effect on memory, courts have not been sympathetic to the recognition of claims of incompetence to stand trial for defendants with amnesia.[31] While not accounting for different individuals' rates of memory decline, statutes of limitations operate as arbitrary limits on memory problems. They presume that the passage of the relevant limitations period reflects the normal decline in the reliability of memory.

There are, however, other difficulties that a defendant may face in cases in which the offense is an old one. In particular, it may be difficult to locate defense witnesses, who may be hard to trace or who may have died. This may affect prosecutors, too; their task of preparing a prosecution of old crimes may be much more time consuming given the difficulties in assembling testimony. From their point of view, then, the limitations rule may have its attractions. In particular, it may allow them to exclude cases that are likely to place an inordinate strain on their time and resources.

If allowing the prosecution of old crimes is unfair to the defendant, then how is the effective absence of a doctrine of limitations justified in Canada and the United Kingdom, which share the same legal tradition as the United States? The Canadian courts have acknowledged that delay may unfairly prejudice a defendant's opportunity for a fair trial, requiring that the prosecution be barred. In general, though, they have been reluctant to conclude that precharge delay has had this effect.[32] The 1997 decision in the case of *MacDonnell* illustrates the response of Canadian courts to such claims.[33] In 1994, a woman in her late 50s was charged with the murder, some 30 years previously, of a 3-year-old boy who had been entrusted to her care. The boy was admitted to hospital with head injuries and died there after neurosurgery. An inquest into his death concluded that death had been caused as a result of two falls. There matters stood until many years later when the defendant's estranged oldest son informed the police that the death of the child had not been accidental, which led to murder charges. By this time, however, both the doctor who treated the child in the hospital and the pathologist who carried out the autopsy had died, and transcripts of their evidence at the inquest were no longer available. The Supreme Court of Canada considered the defendant's claim that the absence of this medical evidence would prejudice her right to a fair trial under the Canadian Charter of Rights and Freedoms but concluded that the likelihood of prejudice had not been proven and permitted the case to proceed to trial.

An even longer period of delay was involved in the *Grandjambe* case, which came before an Alberta court in 1996.[34] This charge concerned events alleged to have taken place more than 40 years earlier. The complainant alleged that in 1954, when she was 11, the defendant, who was then 16, had sexually assaulted her. The defendant contended that it was impossible to defend himself properly against this charge because the destruction of employment records made it impossible for him to establish his alibi. The death of two material witnesses—the defendant's mother and the complainant's mother—denied the defendant evidence in which the complainant's mother was alleged to have accused another person of the offense. In this case this was sufficient to satisfy the court that it would have been unfair to the defendant to proceed with the trial in the face of these substantial obstacles in the way of his defending himself.

The *Grandjambe* case gives us cause to reflect on the dangers of prosecuting substantially delayed allegations of sexual abuse. In that case the defendant's capacity to specify how his ability to defend himself would be compromised persuaded the court to decide in his favor; had he not been able to do this, the decision may well have gone the other way. Justice turned, serendipitously, on the defendant's memory of exculpating events for which other evidence had vanished. The question is whether this imposes an inappropriate burden on the defendant; normally it is reasonable enough to expect a defendant to remember those details of an event that he will need to defend himself, but it may not be reasonable to expect this in the case of events of the distant past. Of course it may be argued that the prosecution is confronted with exactly the same burden in such cases, as the powers of recall of its witnesses may be similarly compromised by the passage of time. In this view, there is no inherent inequity in proceeding to prosecute many years after the event; each case will depend on its merits.

The Canadian discussion of delay in prosecution focuses on the evidential implications and on resulting procedural fairness. In the United Kingdom, where there are also no statutory limitations on prosecutions for serious crimes, the grounds on which a delayed prosecution will be tested is whether it is "oppressive." This notion of oppression is a broad one: It is not restricted to difficulties in getting evidence but looks at the whole circumstances of the prosecution. Implicit in the notion of oppressiveness is the concept of proportionality; in particular, it would be oppressive to seek excessive or unduly harsh punishment. Bringing a delayed prosecution for a minor offense would probably be considered oppressive, not because there is a disparity between the original wrong and the sentence finally imposed, but because it seems harsh to punish in the circumstances. But wherein lies the harshness? Is it the fact that the defendant's life is unduly disrupted, or is it because the disturbance of the defendant's life seems to be excessive? It is a feature of broad criteria—such as oppressiveness—that they do not clarify the extent to which these factors constitute the rationale of the concept. It would therefore seem that what will count will be the extent to which the prosecution strikes the court as "harsh" which, of course, is merely to substitute one general term for another.

Looking for a Civil Remedy

When a statute of limitations prevents a criminal prosecution for a very personal injury, the victim may be inclined to seek a remedy in the civil courts under tort law. This may occur in the case of many sorts of crimes but, for a multitude of reasons, has been particularly prominent in the case of sexual assaults. These assaults are certainly at least as intrusive as any other criminal activity, and they also often involve a breach of trust and a challenge to the victim's identity and self-conception.

In addition, they are unique in the way in which they often subject the victim to social judgment and stigmatization.

Victims may bring claims for a variety of motives. Some litigants may be attracted by the prospect of a financial award; others litigants may be motivated by nonmonetary considerations. Bringing a claim against an abuser holds the potential for self-assertion and vindication. It also provides plaintiffs with an opportunity to hold perpetrators to account for their actions. Even if these goals are not always achieved, it is easy to understand why people bring civil suit in these circumstances, particularly when the defendant is protected from prosecution by criminal limitation provisions.

Although punishment is not a primary goal of tort law, at times it may perform this function. Bringing an action for personal injury is an act of confrontation; it makes inroads on the defendant's time and pocket, and it subjects the defendant to the opprobrium of negative publicity. All of these are features of conventional criminal punishment, even if the punishment falls short of imprisonment. Criminal punishment is intended to humble the convicted person; civil litigation makes a statement about the defendant by exposing the wrong and imposing liability for the payment of damages. Moreover, in some cases in which the defendant's conduct is malicious, the courts may allow the award of punitive damages. The object of such awards is specifically to punish the defendant in the same way as would a fine.

Bringing a claim against a sex abuser engages the victim with the offender. We discuss the therapeutic issues involved in seeking this engagement in chapter 7. Suffice it to say at this point that there are those who encourage bringing these suits, not only for an anticipated healing effect on the plaintiff, but also for the benefit of society as a whole. If these cases are brought, in the full glare of the publicity that tends to surround sexually oriented litigation, the point will be made that sexual abuse will be exposed and abusers will be called to account.

Civil claims, like criminal claims, may be barred by the statute of limitations. Again, the precise limitation period varies from jurisdiction to jurisdiction, but a typical period in the case of a personal injury action is 2 or 3 years (in some states the period is as long as 6 years). In most cases this period will run from the time that the injury is inflicted. In some cases, however, the victim will not be aware of the injury and will discover some years later that he or she has been harmed. An example of this would be cases in which injury is inflicted by a toxic agent; the harmfulness of the exposure may be unknown at the time and may be discovered only after the victim becomes ill or disabled. For this reason, most jurisdictions provide that the limitation period begins to run from the time at which the plaintiff became aware, or should have become aware, of the injury.

There are convincing reasons for insisting that civil claims be brought within a reasonable time.[35] One justification is that the absence of a period of limitations would introduce an unacceptable degree of uncertainty into human affairs. Commercial and industrial concerns need to know the extent of their future liabilities. If there is an ever-present threat that claims from the distant past may surface, financial calculation becomes difficult; a line has to be drawn at some finite point so that accounts may be closed.[36] The same point can be made in relation to technical issues of administration of justice. Civil justice has to work with limited resources, and the litigation of old disputes might edge out more pressing contemporary matters. Apart from these logistic concerns, an important justification for the application of limitations lies in the familiar difficulties associated with stale evidence. We have already seen this difficulty from the point of view of the defendant in a criminal trial; exactly the same problem is present in civil claims. The defendant in a civil claim may find it difficult to raise a proper defense if records have been disposed of or if witnesses are hard to trace.

The exponents of tort claims against sexual abusers do not accept these arguments. They argue that the evidence used in a timely civil action may be fairly old, even before the limitation period has run out.[37] If the limitation period begins to run on the victim's attaining majority—as is usually the case—then a civil suit may competently be brought up to the age of 24 (in the case of a 6-year period). In such a case, if the abusive incidents occurred when the victim was 12, the evidence will be 12 years old, which is hardly recent. Of course, this does not address the objection that 20- or 30-year-old evidence is inherently problematic.

Although the problems of proof presented for defendants are no different in sexual abuse cases and in many regards are worse, other calculations of fairness in applying statutes of limitations weigh differently. The right of repose claimed by defendants—the right not to be exposed to claims from the past—is less compelling in sexual abuse cases. The seriousness of the perpetrator's conduct and its continued effect on the victim outweigh any interest that the perpetrator may have in the avoidance of disruption to his or her life and finances. There is no moral entitlement to write off the consequences of sexual abuse in the same way in which an insurance company might be entitled to write off accident claims that are timely filed. Yet if we accept that the defendant has a claim not to be prosecuted for the crimes of the distant past, as we do for at least some crimes, why should civil obligations be treated differently from criminal liability? If there is a moral duty to forgive after the criminal statute of limitations has run, why should forgiveness of a civil claim not be equally appropriate? Supporters of civil suits might reply that we may be expected to forgive, but the exercise of forgiveness does not preclude obtaining an apology and recompense for suffering. In most cases of civil action against an abuser there will have been no such acknowledgment and no request for forgiveness, which might be one of the main reasons for bringing the suit in the first place.

The Discovery Rule and the Response of the Courts

The discovery rule in the law of torts is designed to help those who have been injured but who are unaware of their injury until after the statute of limitations has run. It provides that if there is good reason for a plaintiff not to have discovered the injury, or its cause, a claim may be brought out of time. Its assistance has therefore been sought by victims of sexual abuse who claim that they were unable to bring suit because of the effect of the abuse. As we have already suggested, sexual abuse constitutes a particular sort of injury because of the magnitude of the harm, the breach of trust involved, and the mistaken belief harbored by some victims of their role in the offense. All of these factors may make it difficult for the victim to acknowledge the offense.

The sexual abuse of children tends by its very nature to be concealed. This is particularly so in cases in which the abuser is a member of the family, but a child victim may also be intimidated by an abuser's threats. Victims who are threatened may not reveal what has happened in a timely manner simply because they are afraid to do so. There are also other factors, however, that may result in delayed disclosure. The spectrum of responses to the trauma of sexual assault ranges from benign to severely disruptive. At the serious end of the spectrum, the responses may include depression, dissociative disorders, suicidal behavior, and difficulties in forming relationships with others. These conditions may make it extremely difficult for the victim to take action to address his or her difficulties, and it may not be until there has been significant therapeutic intervention that the trauma can be confronted and discussed. In some cases, victims may experience denial of the abuse, or they may attempt to trivialize it, thereby failing to make any connection between the fact of the abuse and the psychological consequences being experienced.

There is evidence—admittedly controversial—that one response to sexual abuse is amnesia.[38] The precise mechanism by which this is thought to occur is unclear, but it is generally acknowledged that some survivors of stressful or horrific experiences may have no memory of what happened.[39] What is disputed is whether this memory can later be regained. In chapter 6 we explore in some detail the controversial topic of recovered memory. The nature of recovered memory and its reliability have been the subject of intense and often acrimonious debate, sometimes called the "memory wars."[40] Critics of recovered repressed memory argue that these memories are unreliable.[41] They contend that, in some cases, these memories are created by suggestions made by therapists, and they argue that even if repressed memories may be recovered, there is no way of distinguishing these memories, which may be true, from false memories, which may proceed from outside suggestion or the working of the imagination.

Armed with what they believe to be recovered repressed memories of child sexual abuse, numerous adults have sought redress for what they allege happened to them many years before, but which they have now just remembered. The possibility of bringing criminal charges against the perpetrator is usually excluded in such cases because the period of criminal limitation has expired, but often there remains the possibility of civil suit. Although the limitations periods for civil claims are, as a rule, actually shorter that those for criminal claims, courts have been more flexible in finding exceptions in the case of civil claims for sexual abuse.

The typical vehicle for assisting these plaintiffs in avoiding the application of the statute of limitations is the discovery rule. A classic illustration of this rule is provided by the case of *Ruth v. Dight*.[42] The plaintiff had undergone a hysterectomy in 1944. For the next 22 years she experienced abdominal pain that her physicians could not explain. An exploratory operation was performed in 1966, revealing that a sponge had been left in her abdomen during the earlier procedure, and it was only then that she instituted a lawsuit, long after the statute of limitations for personal injury claims had run. Under these circumstances the court concluded that the plaintiff could not have been expected to discover the cause of her discomfort at an earlier stage—assuming, of course, that she had not unreasonably turned down earlier offers of exploratory procedures. Thus, the court held, the statute of limitations did not begin to run until her discovery of the wrong, and her 22-year-old medical malpractice action was allowed as timely.

Victims of sexual assault frequently claim that they are entitled to benefit from the discovery rule because they had no memory of the abuse when they reached the age of majority and the statute of limitations began to run. Alternatively, they may claim that although they remembered the abuse, they did not realize that it was responsible for their distressing symptoms. Either way, they argue that the delay in bringing a claim is not their fault, and that they should benefit from the discovery rule and be allowed to file a suit well after the normal limitation period has run. The reaction of the courts to this argument has been mixed. The attitude of many courts has been to exclude such claims, but some have allowed them. Moreover, these claims have led to legislative changes to the statute of limitations, specifically to accommodate late actions in these circumstances. Interestingly, the decision both at the judicial and legislative levels to narrow or expand the application of the statute of limitations for these claims has turned on policies devoid of scientific considerations. The courts and legislatures considering limitations questions have rarely examined whether it is scientifically possible that memory can be repressed and then accurately recalled.[43] Instead, these determinations have focused on balancing the interests of plaintiffs and defendants, as if that could be done without addressing the underlying scientific dispute.

One of the earliest repressed-memory discovery rule cases was *Tyson v. Tyson,* a 1986 decision of the Supreme Court of Washington.[44] At the age of 26, the plaintiff, Nancy Tyson, filed a civil claim against her father alleging that he sexually abused her between the ages of 3 and 11. Under the relevant Washington statute, an action for personal injuries must be brought within 3 years of the injury or, in the case of an action for assault or battery, within 2 years of the event. In the case of a wrong committed against a minor, the statute does not begin to run until the victim reaches his or her 18th birthday. Tyson's action was outside the limitation period, but she argued that the discovery rule should be applied because she had only recently recovered the memory of abuse during therapy. The court was skeptical and declined to apply the discovery rule in the absence of independent evidence of abuse.

According to the majority opinion, although therapy might help to treat emotional problems, it was not intended to provide an accurate account of past events.[45] The court thought that the process of uncovering memories of abuse in therapy interjected too many risks of distortion. According to the court, the patient first remembers, then the memory must be expressed or communicated to the therapist, and finally a conclusion must be reached as to the meaning of the memory. The court suggested that this might attenuate the meaning of the original event. Therefore, the court required some objective evidence to confirm the occurrence of the event. In the surgical case in which the discovery rule evolved, the courts did not impose a requirement of objective evidence of the wrong to toll the statute, but in fact such evidence was present: The medical records and scar provided objective evidence of the earlier surgery, and the foreign object used in that surgery that was left in the patient provided objective evidence of the wrong. By contrast, in a recovered-memory case, there may be no evidence of the fact that abuse took place beyond the plaintiff's own disputed recollections. Accordingly, the *Tyson* court declined to apply the discovery rule in these circumstances.

The decision in *Tyson* appeared to foreclose the use of the discovery rule in the absence of corroborating evidence. A distinction has emerged, however, between what are identified as Type 1 and Type 2 cases. In a Type 1 case, the victim claims to have been aware of the abuse all along but has failed to make a causal connection between the fact of the abuse and its adverse consequences. Typically, the victim has recently undergone treatment that has led to an awareness of the relationship of the abuse to some current problem. In a Type 2 case, the victim claims not to have been continuously aware of the abuse, having allegedly just recovered a repressed memory of the incident. Typically, the victim has undergone treatment for an unrelated problem that has led to the discovery of the memory of the abuse.

In general, U.S. courts have been unwilling to apply the discovery rule in Type 1 cases but have been less reluctant to do so in Type 2 cases.[46] This result is surprising, given the scientific doubts surrounding the reliability of recovered repressed memories that surround Type 2 claims but not Type 1 claims. Type 1 claims rely on memories that the plaintiff claims to have possessed continuously since the incident. They pose no special problems of reliability, and the claim that the memories have been consistent over the years may provide some added assurance of reliability. Therefore, the decision to reject Type 1 claims but to permit Type 2 claims turns not on the science of memory, but instead on the law's disapproval of "sleeping on one's rights." In the Type 1 case, the plaintiff is thought to have been capable of bringing a claim, and the law is unwilling to examine the complex reasons why a claim might not have been brought. Considerations of fairness to the defendant loom large in this sort of case. If the plaintiff knew of the wrong, then the defendant is entitled to demand that the claim be brought or abandoned in a timely manner. In the Type 2 case, the plaintiff is not thought to have been capable of bring a claim, and the defendant is correspondingly not entitled to make this demand.

A typical illustration of the American response to a Type 1 case is the Californian decision in *De Rose v. Cardwell*[47] in which the victim claimed to have been aware of the abuse all along, but failed to connect it to her symptoms. The court refused to recognize a discovery rule exception to the strict application of the limitation period on the grounds that the plaintiff was aware of all the "essential facts," including the harmfulness of the original assault. According to the court, it would be different if the wrongful conduct had been less clearly harmful. In such a case, the court assumed, the plaintiff may well be ignorant of its impact.

There are a number of other examples of courts refusing to apply the discovery rule in Type 1 cases. In *E. W. v. D. C. H.*[48] the Supreme Court of Montana refused to apply the rule in a suit brought by a 34-year-old woman who claimed to have been sexually abused by her stepuncle during her childhood. She alleged that the psychological problems from which she suffered as an adult were caused by the abuse, which she had always remembered, but she only began to understand the effect of this abuse once she underwent psychiatric counseling. The court held that the limitation period began to run when she reached the age of majority, at which point she was well aware of the harmful event, even if she did not understand its full implications.

There have been a small number of cases in which the courts have been prepared to apply the discovery rule when the plaintiff has not been able to make the connection between abuse and specific psychological harm. *Hammer v. Hammer*,[49] for example, involved the repeated sexual abuse of a girl by her father when she was between the ages of 5 and 15. Suit was brought 10 years after the abuse ended, at which point the statute of limitations would normally have barred the claim. But the court accepted that the various coping devices that the victim had developed were sufficient to prevent her from making the necessary connection between the abuse and its adverse consequences.

In general, Type 1 cases have met with a more sympathetic response in Canada[50] and New Zealand. One of the more recent such cases is *H. v. R.*,[51] a decision of the

New Zealand High Court. The plaintiff was a man of 35, and the defendant, re-markably, was 88 at the time of the appeal. As a young teenager, the plaintiff had gone with his family to a holiday home on the coast where, over a period of years, he was sexually abused by the defendant, then a man in his 60s. The plaintiff had a troubled adolescence, finding himself in trouble for stealing but also experiencing considerable sexual difficulties, including an inability to achieve orgasm. He sought a confrontation with his abuser but was deflected, and he ended up selling marijuana for his abuser. He went to Australia in his 20s and married there, although the marriage was not a success. In the course of marriage counseling, the counselor raised the subject of sexual abuse, which the plaintiff was unwilling to discuss. Subsequently the plaintiff acknowledged that abuse had taken place, but it was not for a few years that he felt able to take the matter up anew with the defendant and seek legal advice about compensation. The emergence of an intention to seek civil compensation was, therefore, a slow process, even after the plaintiff began to be able to admit to others what had happened. The legal difficulty he faced, though, was that the limitation period for such actions in New Zealand law, 6 years, had expired, even counting from the time at which the plaintiff had reached the age of majority.

The New Zealand court had no difficulty accepting that in cases of sexual abuse a victim might fail to appreciate the causal connection between the abuse itself and later psychological distress. The judge described the plaintiff as a "simple person" who had a borderline personality disorder and who was unable to understand the source of his problems. In these circumstances, the court concluded that the limitation period would not begin to run until the plaintiff understood the effect of the abuse on his life. But the judge went even further than this. If the Limitation Act had run, he said, it might still have been open under New Zealand procedure for the court to issue a declaratory judgment in favor of the plaintiff and award legal costs. The judge acknowledged that the plaintiff wanted recognition of the wrong, rather than money. The judge said

> that is important for him, for all sorts of complex psychosocial reasons; socially; and for his future. . . . Too often common lawyers undervalue the therapeutic and restor-ative value of declaratory orders. That is one of the weak features of our present body of jurisprudence.[52]

The attitude of the courts in both Canada and New Zealand to Type 1 cases appears to condone considerable delay in bringing a claim. The psychological jus-tifications for victims finding it difficult to understand the impact of abuse has per-suaded these courts to be more sympathetic to the interest of the victims than to the rights of the defendants to resolve these claims in a timely fashion. The courts believe, then, that victims may need more time to come to terms with the possibility of an action against the abuser than the legislature has allowed for claimants gen-erally. They see no reason why any interest of the defendant in the timely resolution of the matter should outweigh the victim's need.

A slightly different slant on victim delay is evident in the Australian case of *A. v. D.*[53] The plaintiff in this case alleged that her doctor sexually assaulted her. The assault took place in 1969 and consisted of an unnecessarily long intimate exami-nation, coupled with inappropriate touching. She made a timely complaint to the police and to the medical authorities, but neither of these led to prosecution or professional sanction because of inadequate evidence. A civil claim, under Australian limitations legislation, would have had to be brought within 10 years, but the plaintiff did not initiate proceedings until 1994. This was a substantial delay, but the court took the view that the earlier part of the delay (from 1969 to 1991) could be explained on the basis that the victim was trying to "put the past behind her," and the delay between 1991 and 1994 was caused by her fear that she would not be believed. It was only after she had heard that other patients were making similar allegations against this doctor that she thought that a claim might succeed. Although the court was willing to countenance the victim's delay, the claim was eventually barred on the grounds that it would be impossible for the defendant to bring evidence in his defense; in particular, it would be impossible for him to adduce evidence from people who were in neighboring consulting and waiting rooms at the time of the alleged assault. This potential unfairness to the defendant in the end result outweighed the claims of the victim.

What case can be made for allowing delay in circumstances of this sort? The law has accepted of necessity that the threshold for expecting people to act is knowledge of the possibility of action. Our understanding of human conduct, however, reveals that knowledge of and capacity for action may be distinct. Our ability to act may be affected by a variety of factors, and proponents of Type 1 claims have argued that the courts should recognize those factors and give them legal effect through the application of the discovery rule. They argue that denial frequently follows trauma and that the victim may suppress the memory of what has happened but may also develop a passive attitude toward the experience or take action to avoid confronting what has happened to avoid reawakening the pain. Were this so, it would be understandable that a victim of sexual abuse would seek to isolate the experience and avoid initiating legal action. Bringing a claim may be seen as provoking a recurrence of the traumatic experience. In extreme cases, if posttraumatic stress disorder results, the victim may make deliberate efforts to avoid thinking about the traumatic event or to avoid getting into situations in which recollections of the event will be rekindled.[54] In such circumstances, what might look like simple prevarication or condonation may be a psychological inability to act, springing directly from the original traumatic experience. Viewed in this light, the reluctant litigant might be considered to be under a disability relative to this claim, which should be given some weight.

Even if the science were to support such a notion of the impact of trauma on ability to act, it seems unlikely that the law could accommodate it. It would be impossible for the law to make subjective assessments of each plaintiff's ability to comply with limitation provisions. To do so would introduce an unacceptable element of uncertainty and encourage prolonged litigation. Limitation periods are admittedly arbitrary, and they may seem harsh in the case of traumatized plaintiffs, but they have a sound rationale.

In the United States, the reaction to Type 2 cases has varied, but a number of plaintiffs have successfully argued that the statute of limitations should be tolled for repressed-memory claims. An example of this is *Johnson v. Johnson*,[55] in which the paternal sexual abuse was alleged to have taken place while the plaintiff was between the ages of 3 and 13. The court accepted that the memory of this had been repressed, and that, therefore, the plaintiff's delay in bringing proceedings before a court was attributable to ignorance rather than conscious prevarication.

If repressed memory is not scientifically valid, it seems clear that it should not be an acceptable ground for tolling the statute of limitations. However, if repressed-memory claims are or may be valid, then should they be accepted as grounds for tolling the statute of limitations? If the law accepts, as it generally does, that ignorance of a wrong is a justifiable excuse for not instituting timely legal proceedings, then the victim with a repressed memory is in the same position of ignorance as any other potential plaintiff who is unaware of an injury. Yet in a sense, it is a different sort of ignorance. Repressed-memory proponents do not contend that the plaintiff has never known of the wrong but that the plaintiff has forgotten or repressed the events in question. Forgetting is not normally a ground to excuse bringing an action in a timely manner, except in cases in which the forgetting is the responsibility of the person who caused the initial harm, such as an assault that leads to cognitive impairment. The person inflicting the assault also inflicts the forgetting. Were repressed-memory claims regarded with scientific credibility, in principle, then, repressed memory caused by the defendant's wrongful acts could be grounds for tolling the statute of limitations.

The sharp divisions between social scientists, however, reveal that this is not now the case. Even if there were a sufficient scientific consensus in favor of repressed memory, there are other grounds for caution. The law has to be cautious in dealing with claims that can easily be simulated. It must also be cautious in its response to psychological phenomena that may reflect popular enthusiasms. That there is a high incidence of child sexual abuse is beyond doubt, but society's concern with this should not obscure the possibility that false claims may be made. For this reason, the extension of existing limitation rules to create special categories for these cases may be questionable.

The Case for Limitations

As seen, owing to the willingness of courts to apply the discovery rule more liberally in civil cases than in criminal cases, civil actions are often an alternative for victims even when criminal prosecutions of old crimes are time barred. This is an odd result for several reasons. First, it is odd if we consider the defendant's interests in avoiding the stigma of wrongful punishment that traditionally justifies greater caution in criminal cases than in civil cases. Whereas criminal proceedings hold the possibility of punishment and official condemnation, civil proceedings are, as we discussed, often used by crime victims because they have punitive components and result in a formal legal judgment of responsibility. Civil judgments of responsibility for criminal acts are not benign. Furthermore, it is odd if we consider problems of access to proof, which may pose greater risks to defendants in civil cases in which a finding need only be supported by a preponderance of evidence as contrasted with criminal proceedings in which proof beyond a reasonable doubt is required.

It is also odd, from the point of view of the interests of claimants, that we should permit civil claims when the passage of time bars criminal claims. Why should we be willing to permit a private individual to proceed against a wrongdoer to settle his or her private score when we do not permit the state to proceed to settle the public account? Without denigrating the interests of any individual crime victim, the interests of the state in settling its account on behalf of all of its citizens would seem superior. If this ranking is thought inappropriate, the question arises as to whether the way to rectify it is to apply criminal periods of limitation—which are longer but less flexible—to civil cases. The civil claim in such cases is based on what is, after all, a criminal act. This might satisfy victims who feel that the current limitation periods are too brief in this sort of case.

Certainly, legislatures have tended to agree that longer limitation periods should apply in childhood sexual abuse cases. Recent legislative reforms in a number of states have extended these periods either by reclassifying childhood sexual abuse as a more serious crime or by introducing special rules for this offense. In some cases, reforms have also included the legislative endorsement of a discovery rule. The patterns differ widely, and the difference is politically driven. Some states have settled for a relatively short period after the attainment of majority—2 years in Pennsylvania[56]—whereas others have been extremely generous to the plaintiff. Connecticut gives the plaintiff in a sexual abuse case the most time to bring an action. Under an amendment introduced in 1991, a limitation period of 17 years from the date at which the victim reaches the age of majority applies, thus allowing child sexual abuse claims to be made up to the age of 35.[57]

The radical alternative is to abandon a specific statute of limitations for serious old crimes, treating them as we do murder and responding to claims of unfairness on a case-by-case basis. If the Canadian experience is anything to go by, this approach will likely lead to the imposition of a very high standard for defendants to prove that prosecution is fundamentally unfair. The same experience is reported in Scotland where, although the courts have an inherent power to abate oppressive prosecutions, in practice this power has not been used to prevent the prosecution of old crimes. There is nothing unique about these jurisdictions, and the same pattern applies in other countries where there is no criminal statute of limitations. It seems that it is in practice very difficult for prosecuting authorities and indeed for courts themselves to refrain from allowing a trial when there is an insistent complainant wishing to lay a charge in this highly emotive area of the criminal law.

On balance, the case for both criminal and civil statutes of limitation is compelling. This accords with the argument that we presented in earlier chapters that there comes a point at which the past should no longer dictate our relationships with one another. It also deals with the requirement of forgiveness that we identified in chapter 3. From a practical point of view, limitations ensure that the courts are occupied with recent business to which they can apply satisfactory standards of proof. Limitations keep in check the injustices and unfairnesses that can result if old and unreliable evidence is used. The real policy question then is that of deciding the period of limitations to be applied. This depends on the seriousness of the crime. Sexual offenses are traumatic and should be placed alongside other traumatic offenses such as murder, torture, and kidnapping but should not be unduly privileged.

Endnotes

1. Michael R. Rand, *National Crime Victimization Survey: Carjacking, crime data brief* (Washington, DC: Department of Justice, Office of Justice Programs, Bureau of Justice Statistics, 1994).
2. *Report of the Committee on Sexual Offences Against Children* (Ottawa, Ontario, Canada: Ministry of Supply and Services, 1984).
3. Judith L. Herman, *Father–daughter incest* (Cambridge, MA: Harvard University Press, 1978) at 27.

4. Sandra Butler, *Conspiracy of silence: The trauma of incest* (San Francisco: New Glide, 1978) at 12.

5. J. Don Read and Stephen D. Lindsay, Eds., *Recollections of trauma: Scientific evidence and clinical practice* (New York: Plenum Press, 1997).

6. English law applies limitations in the case of minor, summary offenses. The overwhelming majority of serious offenses are not subject to any limitation (treason being the main exception to this: Under the Treason Act of 1695 a limitation period of 3 years was introduced).

7. For a historical discussion, see "Note. The statute of limitations in criminal law: A penetrable barrier to prosecution," *University of Pennsylvania Law Review* 102 (1954):630–653.

8. *Vernier v. State,* 909 P.2d 1344 (Wyo. 1996).

9. Tex. Code Crim. P. art. 12.01 (1999).

10. Tex. Code Crim. P. art. 12.01 (1998).

11. See Timothy L. H. McCormack, "From Sun Tzu to the Sixth Committee: The evolution of an international criminal law regime." In *The law of war crimes*, Timothy L. H. McCormack and Gerry J. Simpson (Eds.) (The Hague, The Netherlands: Kluwer, 1977) at 31.

12. *Id.*

13. The figure is quoted in *Le Monde*, July 3, 1981.

14. Charles Rousseau, "Chronique des faits internationaux" [Review of international acts], *Revue Generale de Droit International Publique* 96 (1992):873–904.

15. Strafrechtsanderungsgesetz [Criminal law amendment law], *Osterreichisches Bundesgestzblatt* 79 (1965).

16. Alain Finkiekraut, *Remembering in vain: The Klaus Barbie trial and crimes against humanity* (New York: Columbia University Press, 1992).

17. For a full discussion of the *Cour de Cassation's* reasoning, *see* George Desous, "Reflexions sur la regime juridique des crimes contre l'humanite (a propos des arrets Barvie)" [Reactions in the judicial regime over crimes against humanity (particularly with respect to the arrest of Barbie)], *Revue de Sceince Criminelle at de Droit penal Compare* (1984): 657–684.

18. For a full discussion, *see* Leila Sadat Wexler,"The interpretation of the Nuremberg Principles by the French Court of Cassation: From Touvier to Barbie and back again," *Columbia Journal of Transnational Law* 32 (1994):289–380.

19. Commonwealth of Australia, Parl. Deb., H. R., Feb. 24, 1987, col. 595.

20. This case is discussed by Michael D. Kirby, "War crimes prosecution—An Australian update," *Commonwealth Law Bulletin* 19 (1993):781–787. *See*, in general, G. Triggs, "Australia's war crimes trials: All pity choked." In *The law of war crimes*, Timothy L. H. McCormack and Gerry J. Simpson (The Hague, The Netherlands: Kluwer, 1997) at 123.

21. Supreme Court of South Australia, Dec. 22, 1992.

22. See, for example, Rene Cassin and Jean Graven, "Le projet de conventions internationales sur l'impescriptibilite des crimes de guerre et des crimes contre l'humanite [International conventions in telling of the statute of limitations on war crimes and crimes against humanity]." *International Review of Criminal/Penal Law* 37 (1996):375–449.

23. *Convention on the Non-Applicability of Statutory Limitations to War Crimes and Crimes Against Humanity,* opened for signature at New York, Nov. 26, 1968, G.A. Res. 2391, U.N. GAOR, 23d Sess., Supp. No. 18, at 40, U.N. Doc. A/RES/2391 (1968), 754 U.N.T.S. No. 73, 8 I.L.M. 68, entered into force Nov. 1970.

24. *European Convention on the Non-Applicability of Statutory Limitations to Crimes Against Humanity and War Crimes (Inter-European),* signed at Strasbourg, Jan. 25, 1974, Europe. T.S. No. 82, 13 I.L.M. 540, not yet entered into force.

25. *State v. Bently,* 721 P.2d 227 (Kan. 1986).

26. 531 N.E.2d 1151 (Ind. 1989).
27. See, e.g., *State v. Davidson,* 816 S.W.2d 316 (Tenn. 1991).
28. 48 N.W.2d 352 (Minn. 1984).
29. See chapter 6.
30. *Dusky v. United States,* 362 U.S. 402 (1960).
31. Daniel W. Shuman, *Psychiatric and psychological evidence* (2nd ed., Colorado Springs, CO: Shepherds/McGraw-Hill, 1994).
32. For discussion, *see* Tim Quigley, *Procedure in Canadian criminal law* (3rd ed., Scarborough, Ontario, Canada: Carswell, 1997) at 421.
33. *Regina v. MacDonnell,* 1 CAN S.C.R. 305 (1997).
34. *Regina v. Grandjambe,* 108 CCC 3d 338 (1996).
35. For discussion of the rationale of such statutes, see "Note. Developments in the law: Statutes of limitations," *Harvard Law Review* 63 (1950):1177–1269.
36. A rationale espoused in *Order of R. R. Telegraphers v. Railway Express Agency,* 321 U.S. 342, 348 (1944).
37. See discussion in: Gregory G. Gordon, "Comment, adult survivors of childhood sexual abuse and the statute of limitations: The need for consistent application of the delayed discovery rule," *Pepperdine Law Review* 20 (1993):1359–1405.
38. C. M. Roe and M. F. Schwartz, "Characteristics of previously forgotten memories of sexual abuse: A descriptive study," *Journal of Psychiatry & Law* 24 (1996):189–206.
39. This is reflected in dissociative amnesia whose essential feature is "the inability to recall important personal information, usually of a traumatic or stressful nature." *Diagnostic and statistical manual of mental disorders* (4th ed., Washington, DC: American Psychiatric Association, 1994) at 478.
40. Amina Memon and Mark Young, "Desperately seeking evidence: The recovered memory debate," *Legal & Criminological Psychology* 2 (1997):1–24.
41. Peter A. Ornstein, et al. *Reply to the Alpert, Brown & Courtois document: The science of memory and the practice of psychotherapy, American Psychological Association, final report, Working Group on the Investigation of Memories of Childhood Abuse* [APA report] (1996).
42. 453 P.2d 631 (Wa. 1969).
43. Jocelyn B. Lamm, "Note. Easing access to courts for incest victims: Toward an equitable application of the delayed discovery rule," *Yale Law Journal* 100 (1991):2189–2208.
44. 727 P.2d 226 (Wa. 1986).
45. Stuart A. Greenberg and Daniel W. Shuman, "Irreconcilable conflict between therapeutic and forensic roles," *Professional Psychology: Research and Practice* 29 (1997):50–57.
46. Gregory G. Gordon, "Comment. Adult survivors of childhood sexual abuse and the statute of limitations: The need for consistent application of the delayed discovery rule," *Pepperdine Law Review* 20 (1993): 1359–1405.
47. 242 Cal. Reptr. 368 (1987).
48. 754 P.2d 817 (Mont. 1988).
49. 418 N.W.2d 23 (Wisc. 1987).
50. See Natalie Des Rosiers, "Limitation periods and civil remedies for childhood sexual abuse," *Canadian Family Law Quarterly* 9 at 43 (1992).
51. *H. v. R., New Zealand Law Review* 1 at 299 (1996).
52. *Id.*
53. (Unreported)Supreme Court of the Australian Capital Territory, Sept. 20, 1995.
54. American Psychiatric Association, *Diagnostic and statistical manual of mental disorders* (4th ed., Washington, DC: American Psychiatric Association, 1994).
55. 766 F.Supp. 662 (Ill. 1991).
56. *Dalrymple v. Brown,* 701 A.2d 164 (Pa. 1997).
57. Conn. Gen. Stat. Sec. 52–577d (1997).

Chapter 5
OLD CRIMINALS AND CRIMES:
Pardon and Amnesty in the Prosecution of Old Crimes

Most criminal wrongdoing can give rise to a civil damage claim. For example, murder and sexual assault are intentional wrongs that give rise to a claim for battery; injury sustained as the result of another's driving under the influence of alcohol gives rise to a claim for negligence. Unlike the decision to institute criminal prosecution, however, whether the defendant has assets or liability insurance typically plays an important role in whether a civil action is brought. As seen in chapter 4, adults who engage in child abuse may be prosecuted for their criminal wrongdoing and civilly sued for the harm that they have caused. Of course, in cases in which the abuse is attributed to the negligence of a church or day-care center, the financial incentive to bring a civil claim may be greater than in cases in which the abuse is solely attributed to an individual. The same may be said for drunk drivers covered by liability insurance, who may be sued for the damage they have caused and prosecuted for their criminal wrongdoing. It is informative to examine the differences in these civil and criminal proceedings arising out of the same acts to see how they transform the role of the injured party in these proceedings.

The Unique Nature of Criminal Proceedings

Civil damage claims are brought in the name of the person harmed, but crimes are prosecuted in the name of the state. The pleadings in a civil action and the label that is used to identify the case begins with the name of the person harmed, but criminal proceedings begin with the name of the governmental entity authorized to bring the prosecution. Only the defendant's name personalizes the label of the criminal case. Unlike civil actions, criminal case names do not identify the person that the defendant harmed.

Civil and criminal cases also differ fundamentally in what they regard as the underlying harm. Tort claims, whether they arise out of unintentional, negligent conduct—such as automobile accidents, medical malpractice, or the sale of defective products—or whether they arise from intentional conduct—such as assault or abuse—are regarded as a wrong against the person harmed by the tortious conduct. Thus, subject to the substantive law of the relevant jurisdiction, an accident, abuse, or torture victim may decide unilaterally whether to bring a civil damage claim against the person or institution who has caused the harm and may make a series of tactical decisions, such as whether to settle the case or proceed to trial. A victim of assault or abuse, however, may not decide unilaterally whether to bring a criminal prosecution. That decision, and related tactical decisions, such as whether to accept a plea bargain or to proceed to trial, are the state's. Criminal acts are regarded as a wrong against the state.

Although there has been increased sensitivity to the plight of victims, the effect of the criminal justice system on them, and the desire of victims to have a voice in the criminal justice system in the latter part of the 20th century, the fundamental distinction in the role of the individual victim in civil and criminal proceedings remains.[1] These distinctions are not inadvertent. Crime is formally regarded as a harm to the state that proscribed the criminal act. Practically, reserving to the state the exclusive power to punish is regarded as an important means of halting the spiral of violence that might otherwise result if victims were free to pursue private vengeance and retaliation. In addition, as criminal acts threaten the emotional and physical security of the community, the state has an interest in punishment that extends beyond the punishment preferences of individual crime victims or their survivors.

Giving the state the exclusive power to punish has important implications not only for the decision to institute punishment, but also for the decision to abate punishment. An adult who was sexually abused as a child by her father may choose whether to forgive him or to institute or settle a civil damage claim. However, whatever psychological or moral consequence an act of forgiveness or the institution or settlement of a civil damage claim may have for the victim and the criminal, it has no direct legal consequence in the criminal justice system. The victim's forgiveness, settlement, or pursuit of a civil damage claim is irrelevant to an abuser's criminal culpability. Only the state's forgiveness, manifested through a grant of clemency, directly affects the imposition of punishment. Thus, just as it is important to ask whether the passage of time in itself makes victim forgiveness in the form of a grant of clemency imperative (see chapter 3), so too, it is important to ask whether the passage of time in itself makes state forgiveness similarly imperative.

Granting Clemency

The power of the state to grant clemency to both accused and convicted wrongdoers is widely acknowledged and is recognized throughout the world.[2] Indeed, it is difficult to imagine a criminal justice system without the power to grant clemency. Whether clemency is used to redress injustice or to alleviate prison overcrowding, the operation of the modern criminal justice system would be dramatically altered without it.

A grant of clemency make take many forms. A pardon is usually granted to individuals after they have been sentenced. In its broadest form, a pardon "releases the punishment and blots out of existence the guilt, so that in the eye of the law the offender is as innocent as if he had never committed the offense."[3] *Amnesty* is usually granted to groups of people prior to their trial, and its effect is to forget or overlook the offense.[4] *Commutation* is a postsentence grant that substitutes a lesser punishment for the one imposed.[5] *Remission of fine* is a postsentence grant that returns or forgives the payment of fines. *Reprieve* is a postsentence grant that temporarily suspends the imposition of punishment.[6] Although pardon, amnesty, commutation, remission, and reprieve are separate and distinct forms of clemency that express different notions of forgiveness, in practice the distinctions between them are often not carefully observed. Newspaper stories or statements of public officials are often misleading about the form of clemency exercised, using pardon generically to refer to all grants of clemency.

The processes that result in punishment and clemency are fundamentally different. The decision to punish is the collaborative, albeit often uncoordinated, decision of a cast of actors in the criminal justice system—the police, prosecutors, judges, and jurors—enforcing criminal laws enacted by the legislature and approved by the chief executive. Some of these actors, such as the legislature, chief executive, jurors, and popularly elected judges, are chosen as representatives of the community. Some, such as the police, prosecutors, and appointed judges, are chosen for their criminal justice expertise. Punishment occurs only when the decisions of all of these actors concur.

To see how this concurrence must operate for punishment to occur, consider the decision whether to punish a person for engaging in an extramarital affair, adultery. Although adultery remains a crime in many states, today it rarely results in criminal punishment. Although many state legislatures have retained adultery as a crime,[7] the police rarely investigate allegations of it, prosecutors rarely prosecute it, and juries rarely convict defendants of it. Because the decisions of all of the important decision makers in the criminal justice process rarely concur in favor of prosecution of adultery, punishment, however publicized,[8] is rare. The legislature, police, prosecutor, and jury must all agree that adultery is a criminal act that occurred and should be punished in this instance for punishment to occur. If any one of these actors disagrees that an act is criminal and should result in punishment, punishment will not occur.

In contrast with the collaborative decision to punish, the exercise of clemency is principally an executive decision. The power to grant clemency is typically vested in the jurisdiction's highest elected official. The power to pardon federal offenses is held by the U.S. President, just as the power to pardon state offenses is typically held by the governor, although in many jurisdictions this power is subject to the advice or approval of a pardon board or, rarely, the legislature.[9] Acts of clemency, which are inherently unilateral, invariably reverse or frustrate the collective decisions of the legislature, police, prosecutors, judges, and jurors. In one telling protest of the antidemocratic nature of clemency, in the immediate aftermath of the 1789 French Revolution, the power to pardon was abolished as an antidemocratic institution because it frustrated the legislative will of the people.[10] Why should clemency ever be granted when it frustrates the democratic principles imbedded in the normal operation of the criminal justice system, and if it should be granted, what limits should be placed on it?

Surprisingly, given the antidemocratic potential of a grant of clemency, subject to procedural rules that govern the manner of conducting clemency inquiries, there are few limitations on clemency, particularly insofar as postconviction activity is concerned. The one common limitation on the exercise of clemency power is in the case of the crimes of treason and impeachment.[11] Otherwise, clemency power is largely unrestricted. Unfortunately, history provides no solace that unrestricted clemency power will invariably be exercised wisely. "Given the relationship of clemency to conceptions of justice, it is surprising that clemency has not historically been exercised in any principled way."[12] History reveals both principled examples of grants of clemency designed to achieve just results and unprincipled grants of clemency sold or doled out to repay political debts. For example, between 1915 and 1917, Governor James Ferguson of Texas made vast sums pardoning 1,774 prisoners before he was impeached.[13] Oklahoma Governor J. C. Walton was impeached in 1926 for selling hundreds of pardons.[14] In the 1980s, Tennessee Governor Ray Blanton was prosecuted following a scandal involving the sale of pardons.[15]

Clemency, inherently controversial even in "easy" cases, is often at the heart of dramatic social change and transition. The proponents of clemency argue that, judiciously exercised, clemency holds the power to heal a troubled people, whereas its critics argue that it frustrates justice that is necessary for healing. Consider three controversial pardons granted by U.S. Presidents—Gerald Ford's post-Watergate pardon of Richard Nixon, Jimmy Carter's post-Vietnam War pardon of draft evaders, and Abraham Lincoln's post-Civil War pardon of confederate soldiers. President Ford justified his pardon of Nixon as an effort to help heal the national wounds that Watergate had caused, just as President Carter justified his grant of amnesty for those who had evaded compulsory military service as an effort to help heal the national wounds from the Vietnam War.[16] These more recent controversial uses of clemency intended to heal national wounds are not unique in American history. President Lincoln justified a grant of amnesty for those who took up arms against the Union as an effort to help heal the national wounds that the Civil War had inflicted.[17]

This pattern of controversial grants of clemency to help heal national wounds has been repeated around the globe, although the source of these amnesties has varied. In South Africa, amnesties have been granted for crimes committed in support of and in opposition to apartheid by the Truth and Reconciliation Commission created by the National Unity and Reconciliation Act passed by the South African National Assembly.[18] In Uruguay, the "impunity law" granting amnesty to members of the armed forces and the police for crimes committed during the war under the 1973–1985 military dictatorship was approved in a national referendum.[19] In Argentina, the president pardoned members of the military dictatorship in the war against leftists in the 1970s that resulted in the abduction and disappearance of 30,000 people.[20] In Chile, General Pinochet imposed an amnesty as a condition of stepping down from power, thus protecting members of the military who ruled Chile from 1973 to 1990 when thousands of opponents of the government were killed and tortured.[21]

The justifications offered for these grants of amnesty have been remarkably similar. The amnesty granted through the South African Truth and Reconciliation Commission was justified as a necessary step in national healing and reconciliation. In Argentina, Chile, and Uruguay, successor regimes that replaced repressive regimes responsible for the disappearance of thousands of citizens instituted various amnesties that they justified as necessary to encourage national unity or to avoid confrontation with the military. We have already seen in chapter 1 that many of these acts of clemency have provoked considerable criticism that justice and restoration of the moral balance in society are ill served by these grants of clemency. Critics argue that granting clemency will only encourage similar crimes and ultimately undermine these fledgling democracies. Claims that clemency was necessary to permit the country to heal its wounds and move beyond these events have been matched with claims by a campaign against impunity[22] that these laws mocked victims and ignored the gravity of their suffering. Human rights groups have sharply criticized grants of amnesty in South Africa as a betrayal of the victims of violence. In addition, many families of those killed during apartheid, like the family of student activist Steve Biko, have strongly opposed amnesty.[23] In Argentina, Chile, and Uruguay, victims have expressed the persistent fear that they will inadvertently come across in the street the person who tortured them. Just as there is much interesting theory but no proof of the therapeutic consequences of criminal prosecution (see chap. 7), so too there is interesting theory but no proof of the therapeutic consequences of these acts of clemency. The preliminary evidence of the effect of the Truth and Reconciliation Commission approach is that, for the individual victims of these regimes, psychological healing has not matched the benefits of a stable social transformation. "To ensure stability, the interests of the nation have been placed before those of individuals."[24] It may well be that in situations like South Africa, it was necessary to forgo demands for formal justice, but whatever national benefit is achieved through this approach may come at the cost of individual psychological healing.[25]

All of these major amnesties involve offenses on a large scale. We now turn to individual crimes that do not necessarily form part of a widespread program of oppression. The most obvious and arguably least controversial ground to consider a principled exercise of clemency, evidence bearing on the prisoner's innocence, is not the focus of this chapter. Instead, given our focus on the prosecution of old crimes, we address clemency, typically in the form of pardon or amnesty, in cases in which the passage of time raises questions of the justness of punishment. Thus, we address cases in which criminals were justly prosecuted, convicted, and sentenced or justly should have been prosecuted and convicted in timely fashion but were not, where the passage of time now has a bearing on the justness of the imposition of punishment. We are concerned here not only with criminals who were long ago convicted and are still confined, but also with criminals who long ago committed acts for which they have yet to be punished.

Clemency and the Passage of Time

The effect of the passage of time on the justness of continued punishment is a permissible and appropriate ground for the exercise of discretion to grant clemency.[26] Although there are good grounds for proceeding cautiously and skeptically, decisions to punish made in the distant past may not reflect the reality of the world in which, many years later, the decision is made to continue punishment. Changes occurring in both the criminal and the society that criminalized that conduct may justify reconsideration of the continued desirability of punishment.

One important ground for imposing punishment is to incapacitate dangerous criminals and protect society from them. The passage of time and its effect on a criminal may appropriately cause the state to reconsider the necessity to confine a criminal to protect society or to rehabilitate him or her. Even criminals who are rightly regarded at sentencing as violent, dangerous, and beyond hope of change may change or may be changed by age, illness, disease, or disability. Although these cases may be the exception rather than the rule, some prisoners do undergo radical transformations during their confinement. Stories like that of David Ramos, a convicted murderer who has taught more than 1,000 inmates to read, are not unheard of.[27] Yet we are, with good justification, inherently skeptical of the validity of these claims of criminal transformations, fearing that they are false or, at best, that they reflect superficial transitory changes motivated by a desire for early release. Reflecting society's skepticism, pardons based on jailhouse religious conversions and repentance, for example, are rarely, if ever, granted.

We return here to the case of Karla Faye Tucker, the former prostitute and drug dealer who, along with her boyfriend, was convicted and sentenced to be executed in Texas for a brutal pick-ax murder of her ex-lover and his companion while they

slept during a 1983 break-in to steal motorcycle parts. Tucker never denied responsibility for the crime and apparently underwent a religious transformation on death
row, where she became a model prisoner, repented for her crimes, and played an
active role in the prison ministry. Tucker's request for clemency focused on her
transformation over the 15 years since the crime. Ultimately, the Texas Board of
Pardons and Parole, along with the governor, rejected her claim for clemency, finding
it irrelevant to her death sentence for these brutal murders, and Tucker was executed
in 1998.[28]

Perhaps this skepticism in the face of jailhouse transformations reflects a realistic
understanding of the population of the nation's prisons or perhaps it reflects a political reality in which there is little to be gained and much to be lost by an elected
official who takes a chance on granting clemency to a convicted criminal.[29] At least
recently, at the level of federal crimes, the exercise of clemency based on a transformation of a criminal has been more common in the case of criminals who have
completed their term of confinement, have not returned to a life of crime, and seek
to remove this black mark from their record. Presidents Ronald Reagan, George
Bush, and Bill Clinton continued the policy of their recent predecessors to consider
pardons only for federal offenders who have served their full sentence and who have
thereafter maintained a clean record for 5–7 years.[30]

One of the most common consequences of the passage of time on the use of
clemency is the effect of age, illness, disease, or disability on the necessity of continued confinement to incapacitate a once dangerous criminal. For example, 26 states
provide for some form of compassionate release for terminally ill inmates, and others
may choose to factor this into a particular case pragmatically.[31] The exercise of this
power varies greatly from state to state; over time, in some states, it plays a major
role in the exercise of clemency. One review of Washington state pardons revealed
that 6 out of 10 prisoners pardoned by the governor during one year had a terminal
illness.[32] Of the 2,500 clemency applications made to Governor Mario Cuomo of
New York between 1983 and 1992, he granted only 29 and, of those, ill health was
the explanation for 6.[33]

The principled basis for granting a pardon or commutation to a prisoner who
has changed or who has been changed by age, illness, disease, or disability is the
absence of the need for confinement to protect society. Criminals who are truly
rehabilitated or so debilitated that they lack the capacity to engage in criminal conduct no longer pose the same risk of criminal behavior that may once have served
to justify their confinement. There may be, however, other compelling justifications
for punishment unrelated to the risk of criminal conduct. The retributive justification
for punishment—redressing the moral balance that is disturbed by the commission
of a crime—is unaffected by the necessity to confine the prisoner to protect society.
Consider, for example, the 1982 decision of the World War II Allies to continue to
confine Rudolph Hess, Hitler's military architect, in Spandau prison at the age of
92. Hess was convicted at the Nuremberg Tribunal in 1947 of preparing a war of
aggression and committing crimes against peace, and he was sentenced to a life term
of imprisonment. The justification for the decision to continue to confine Hess rests
more sensibly on the importance of acknowledging the harm that Hess caused than
on the conduct he might engage in if released from prison at the age of 92.[34] Thus,
the decision to continue to confine Hess is a compelling example of why a state may
sensibly wish to continue to punish a criminal on retributive grounds who appears

to lack the capacity to engage in the criminal conduct that resulted in the confinement (see also chap. 7).

Moreover, there are also therapeutic arguments for opposing clemency unrelated to the risk of ongoing criminal conduct. A pardon freeing an elderly or disabled prisoner who committed a crime in the distant past, which seems unlikely to be repeated, may nonetheless have a profound antitherapeutic effect on the victim. For example, when the Netherlands pardoned two Nazi war criminals in 1989 who had been convicted for their role in the death of 10,000 Dutch Jews, Holocaust survivors protested that the release caused survivors a great deal of suffering.[35] Similarly, in long-delayed child sexual abuse prosecutions, there are numerous retributive and therapeutic justifications for punishment unaffected by the passage of time. Even if time has rehabilitated or disabled a person convicted of child molestation, continued confinement of him or her may help to deter other molesters, provide a therapeutic salve for the victim, or restore the moral balance that was disturbed by the crime. Thus, although the passage of time may reduce the risk of a convict's recidivism, the case for granting clemency to a prisoner who has changed or who has been changed by age, illness, or disability must be weighed against the utilitarian, therapeutic, and retributive justifications for continued punishment.

The passage of time, and its effect on society, may also cause the state to grant clemency based on a reconsideration of the wrongfulness of the conduct for which the prisoner was convicted. With the passage of time, the social and political contexts that shaped society's perspective on the conduct may change. Acts that were once soundly condemned may later find social acceptance or political support. Whereas some acts, such murder and theft, are consistently condemned by the criminal law, our attitude toward others acts may change, often sharply.[36]

A striking example of such a change in social and political contexts is the American experience with the passage of Prohibition, a constitutional amendment outlawing the manufacture, sale, or transportation of intoxicating liquors in 1919, and its repeal in 1933.[37] After the repeal of Prohibition, the formal change in attitudes about alcohol resulted in pardons being granted for those who had been convicted of violations of liquor laws.[38] Repeal of Prohibition justified reconsideration of the confinement of prisoners who had violated the repealed Prohibition laws. Another example of a policy change is the U.S. involvement in the Vietnam War. One interpretation of President Carter's grant of amnesty to those who evaded compulsory military service is that, viewed through the post-Vietnam War lens, these acts were an important step in forcing the country to reconsider its involvement in that war, or were at least morally ambiguous. More recently, in the early 1990s, reflecting a set of changing attitudes about domestic abuse, the governors of Ohio and Maryland granted clemency to more than 30 women who had been convicted of killing their batterers,[39] and the New York Assembly passed a resolution asking the governor to order the Division of Parole to consider the cases of women convicted of killing their abusing spouses.[40]

Of course, in cases in which the conduct in question is or should be as resoundingly condemned today as at the time of its commission, there is no compelling reason to consider a grant of clemency based on a reassessment of the wrongfulness of that conduct. For example, because military execution of innocent civilians as a reprisal during wartime is just as heinous now as it was 50 years ago, on this basis there should be no reason to consider a grant of clemency to Erich Priebke for his execution of Italian civilians during World War II.[41] Similarly, the acts of theft in which Ronald Biggs and his partners in crime engaged in the Great Train Robbery in 1962 are now as resoundingly condemned by society as they were then.[42] Our attitudes about theft have not changed. Thus, in reconsidering the wrongfulness of the conduct, there is no basis to consider granting clemency now to Biggs. Although many people have supported clemency for Biggs purely on the grounds that this crime took place so long ago, this attitude lacks a principled basis. In the case of some crimes—for example, child abuse—society's condemnation today is undoubtedly stronger than it was several decades ago. Thus, there is no reason to consider a grant of clemency based on a reassessment of the wrongfulness of that conduct. Instead, only where time has changed society's perspective on these acts would a grant of clemency based on reconsideration of the wrongdoing of the conduct be appropriate.

Additionally, psychological insights and discoveries gained with the passage of time may cause the state to reconsider the utility or desirability of punishment. This has happened in the case of many of the 300 British soldiers summarily court martialed and shot for cowardice or desertion during the horrific trench warfare battles of World War I. As pointed out in chapter 1, the British government ultimately turned down the request for a posthumous pardon. An important aspect of the debate regarding these soldiers and the propriety of granting posthumous pardon was our understanding of posttraumatic stress disorder, formally recognized as a mental disorder in 1980,[43] and the effect of the trauma of war on those caught up in it.[44] Consideration of granting this posthumous pardon reflects, in part, on evolving research about the effect of the psychological trauma of combat and, in part, on evolving standards of military justice.

Critics of the attempt to secure a posthumous pardon for these soldiers argued that it was inappropriate to reopen the decisions of past tribunals on the ground that we would today have reached a different decision on the issues before them. They argued that justice had been done according to the standards of the day and the fact that these standards had changed in light of advances in the study of human behavior was not sufficient justification for disturbing the settled result. The suggestion was made that this was an attempt to rewrite history.

It would have been different, of course, were there living victims of an injustice. Of course the case for pardon is strengthened if the victim of the injustice is still alive. In such a case the state has an unquestionable duty to set the record right and to restore the reputation of the wrongly convicted prisoner. Clearly, in such a case a retrospective examination of a conviction may be justified; one is in a position to rectify a past wrong and to relieve current unjustified suffering. In this case the families claimed that they were victims for whom the injustice of the summary court martial and execution for cowardice or desertion remained. The rejection of a posthumous pardon for these soldiers regards the claims of their descendants, few of whom were born when these events occurred, as too attenuated to be legally cognizable.

The case for a posthumous pardon may be made with two ends in view. There were living interests involved: Relatives of the executed men felt distress for what they saw as a wrong to a member of their family. These are current feelings that could make some claim for our recognition. At a more general level, a posthumous pardon may be seen as a rectification. Historical accuracy is important, and if we misunderstand the past then we should perhaps rectify our vision of it. By granting posthumous pardons to these soldiers, the state would be implicitly committing itself to a different view of their conduct. Such a commitment may have great significance for the present. The state would effectively be saying that it understands that conduct of this sort may be blameless, and it is implicitly undertaking to bear this understanding in mind in its future dealing with its citizens. The moral quality of the state may be improved by a frank confrontation with the past. By owning up to a past wrong, even if the victim of the wrong is no longer present, the state declares its moral position. Rewriting history is an act of self-acknowledgment. A posthumous pardon is a means by which this self-acknowledgment may be given a particular, identifiable form. We understand it because it is so personal—it talks about a particular person and deed.

Considerations

What, then, are the factors that press for clemency after the passage of time? The following considerations seem to be important: a diminution of the risks that the criminal poses to society as the result of the prisoner's advancing age, illness, or disability; significant changes in the social or political context of the society in which the prisoner was convicted; and significant changes in scientific or other knowledge that shape the way in which the conduct is viewed. Even when the passage of time presents compelling reasons to consider a grant of clemency, these reasons must nonetheless be balanced against the countervailing considerations. The nature of the crime for which the criminal was convicted may demand continued retribution without regard to the risk that the criminal poses of reoffending. Apart from the risks to society at large, clemency may have a profound antitherapeutic consequence to a victim that a caring society should not ignore.

Endnotes

1. *New directions from the field victims' rights and services for the 21st century* (Washington, DC: U.S. Dept. of Justice, Office of Justice Programs, Office for Victims of Crime, 1998); Kent Roach, *Due process and victims' rights: The new law and politics of criminal justice* (Toronto, Ontario, Canada: University of Toronto Press, 1999).
2. Leslie Sebba, "Criminology: The pardoning power—A world survey," *Journal of Criminal Law & Criminology* 68 (1977):83–110, at 85.
3. *Ex parte* Garland, 71 U.S. (4 Wall.) 333, 380 (1867).
4. *Burdick v. United States,* 236 U.S. 79 (1915).
5. *Schick v. Reed,* 419 U.S. 256, 273 n8 (1974) (Marshall, J., diss.).
6. *Ex parte* United States, 242 U.S. 27 (1916).
7. See, e.g., Alabama Code § 13A-13-2 (1998); Arizona Revised Statutes § 13-1408 (1998); Colorado Revised Statutes § 18-6-501 (1997).
8. William J. Bennett, "Adultery by political candidates can be relevant," *Milwaukee Journal Sentinel*, Mar. 15, 1999, Monday final, at 10 (describing the adulterous affairs, unprosecuted, of President William Clinton, former President Franklin Roosevelt, former Senator Gary Hart, and Representative Henry Hyde).

9. Christen Jensen, *The pardoning power in the American states* (Chicago: University of Chicago Press, 1922).
10. Kathleen Dean Moore, *Pardons: Justice, mercy, and the public interest* (New York: Oxford University Press, 1989).
11. Jensen, *Pardoning power,* at 32.
12. Daniel T. Kobil, "The quality of mercy strained: Wresting the pardoning power from the king," *Texas Law Review* 69 (1991):569–641, at 572.
13. "Note. Executive clemency in capital cases," *New York University Law Review* 39 (1964): 136–192, at 141 n. 25.
14. Linda L. Ammons, "Discretionary justice: A legal and policy analysis of a governor's use of clemency power to punish in cases of incarcerated battered women," *Journal of Law and Policy* 3 (1994):1–79, at 25.
15. Christine Noelle Becker, "Clemency for killers? Pardoning battered women who strike back," *Loyola of Los Angeles Law Review* 29 (1995):297–342, at 311.
16. Exec. Order No. 11,967, 3 C.F.R. § 91 (1978).
17. A presidential proclamation (May 29, 1865), reprinted in six compilations of the messages and papers of the presidents (1789–1895) at 310.
18. See chapter 1.
19. "Amnesty for military retained," *Facts on File World News Digest*, Apr. 21, 1989, at 294 E3.
20. "Argentine president pardons more military and civilians," *Reuters*, Oct. 19, 1989, Thursday, AM cycle.
21. Carlos Castilho, "The open wound of the disappeared," *Inter Press Service*, May 18, 1996.
22. *Campaign against impunity: Portrait and plan of action* (Montreal, Quebec, Canada: International Centre for Human Rights and Democratic Development, 1997).
23. David Yutar and Beauregard Tromp, "South Africa; The Biko, Benzien amnesty poser," *Africa News Service, Inc.*, Feb. 22, 1999.
24. Brandon Hamber, *Who pays for peace? Implications of the negotiated settlement for reconciliation, transformation and violence in a post-apartheid South Africa.* (Johannesburg, South Africa: Centre for the Study of Violence and Reconciliation, 1988).
25. Brandon Hamber and Richard Wilson, *Symbolic closure through memory, reparation and revenge in post-conflict societies* (Johannesburg, South Africa: Centre for the Study of Violence and Reconciliation, 1998). There is reason for concern about the broader impact of the Truth and Reconciliation Commission (TRC) as well. One survey of White South Africans revealed that a majority have been unconvinced by the TRC that they played a role in apartheid abuses. Gunnar Theisen and Brandon Hamber, "A state of denial: White South Africans' attitudes to the Truth and Reconciliation Commission," *Indicator South Africa* 15(1) (1998):8–12.
26. See Moore, *Pardons.*
27. Jennifer Warren, "Inmate serving 26 to life is state's top literary tutor," *LA Times*, Mar. 9, 1998, at A1.
28. "Face to face with Jesus: After a long and passionate debate, Karla Faye Tucker goes to her death," *Time*, Feb. 16, 1998, at 157.
29. See, e.g., Robert E. Pierre, "Setting the bait: Same tactic, other party," *The Washington Post*, Nov. 15, 1998, Sunday, final ed., Outlook sec., at C2 (discussing the Republican attack on Democratic presidential candidate Michael Dukakis during the 1988 campaign, for his parole of Willie Horton, a convicted murderer who raped a woman while on furlough, while Dukakis was Governor of Massachusetts).
30. 28 C.F.R. § 1.2 (1998).
31. Ira Robbins, *Prisoners and the law* (Deerfield, IL: Clark Boardman Callaghan, 1993).
32. Susan Gilmore, "Clemency is granted most often to those with terminal illness," *The Seattle Times*, June 6, 1996, at A18.

33. Edward Adams, "Cuomo faces annual ritual of deciding on clemency," *New York Law Journal*, Dec. 28, 1992, at 1.
34. "Kohl appeals to four powers to free Rudolph Hess," *Reuters North African Service*, Aug. 1, 1986, PM cycle.
35. Paul Verschuur, "Netherlands pardons Nazi war criminals after 43 years in jail," *Associated Press*, Jan. 27, 1989.
36. See, Richard L. Gray, "Note. Eliminating the (absurd) distinction between *malum in se* and *malum prohibitum* crimes," *Washington University Law Quarterly* 73 (1995):1369–1398 (describing the history of the law's attempt to distinguish between crimes that are *malum in se*, acts regarded as evil in itself, and crimes that are *malum prohibitum*, acts regarded as prohibited evils).
37. U.S. Constitution Amendment 21 § 2: "The transportation or importation into any State . . . for delivery or use therein of intoxicating liquors, in violation of the laws thereof, is hereby prohibited."
38. Moore, *Pardons*, at 158.
39. Cathryn Creno, "Do 'victims' who kill deserve relief?" *Arizona Republic*, Mar. 23, 1993, at E1.
40. Edward Adams, "Cuomo faces annual ritual of deciding on clemency," *New York Law Journal*, Dec. 28, 1992, at 1.
41. Celestine Bohlen, "Italy opens trial in wartime massacre in Rome," *New York Times,* Dec. 8, 1995, at A4.
42. Katherine Ellison, "Where justice stops at the border: Fugitives find sanctuary in South America," *The Miami Herald,* Dec. 27, 1997, International News Sec.
43. American Psychiatric Association, *Diagnostic and statistical manual of mental disorders* (3rd ed. rev., Washington, DC: Author, 1987)
44. "U.K. may pardon shot WWI 'traitors'," *Toronto Star,* May 28, 1997, at A21.

Chapter 6
REMEMBRANCE OF CRIMES PAST:
Memory and Truth Finding in the Prosecution of Crimes

> We have an incapacity of truth, unsurmountable by all dogmatism. We have an idea
> of truth, immutable to all skepticism.[1]

The concept of justice in the prosecution of criminal charges means many different things to different people. To some, justice invokes consideration of retribution, visiting appropriately severe punishment on those who cause harm by violating the rights of others.[2] To others, justice invokes considerations of mercy and rehabilitation and seeks to understand and promote change in the behavior of those who do not abide by society's norms.[3] Yet to others, justice should be concerned with the plight of victims, and they call for the criminal justice system to be used as a therapeutic tool to aid the recovery of victims.[4]

However one conceives of justice, a common thread running through most conceptions is a concern with ascertaining the truth, accurately sorting out the facts that are relevant to a criminal charge.[5] Although truth finding is certainly not the only consideration in just criminal proceedings—and it may at times compete with important considerations of consistency, efficiency, or cost—truth finding nonetheless remains an important transcendent concern. Inaccurate fact finding may result in the guilty avoiding deserved punishment or, worse still, the innocent receiving undeserved punishment. It may also have other important social consequences. Inaccuracy undermines the deterrent function of the criminal law and the state's moral authority to punish. People cannot be expected to regard punishment as a deterrent to unlawful activities or to accept the state's moral authority to punish unless punishment is rendered when people commit unlawful acts and only on them. If punishment is imposed unpredictably and unreliably without regard to what people have actually done, why should people bother to conform their conduct to legal norms? Given this justifiable concern with accuracy in the criminal justice system, a core question in the prosecution of old crimes is the effect of the passage of substantial time between the act and the trial on the ability to reach an accurate determination of the relevant facts.

This chapter discusses the research on memory that plays a role on the ability to reach accurate factual determinations in the prosecution of old crimes. It addresses memory generally, relevant differences in adult's and children's memories, as well as the effect that the horrific events that are often the subject of delayed prosecution may have on memory. Finally, we address the evidence in particularly long-delayed prosecutions presented by recovered-memory claims and recent attempts to prosecute crimes committed during World War II.

Research on Memory

Accurate reconstruction of past events is problematic in the prosecution of all crimes.[6] Accordingly, the criminal justice system requires that the jury and judge be highly confident in the correctness of their fact finding. Although the beyond-a-reasonable-doubt standard of persuasion that applies in criminal cases does not demand absolute certainty, it does demand a very high degree of confidence in the accuracy of the fact-finding process.[7] Achieving this level of certainty is often problematic for the criminal justice system. Criminals normally seek to avoid detection or identification. Even in the case of timely prosecution of recent crimes, it will rarely, if ever, be possible to be 100% certain about what really happened.[8] Recording equipment is not normally in place to memorialize criminal events. There is rarely a signal to prospective witnesses to pay close attention to the events that are to follow because they will one day be the subject of a criminal prosecution. Furthermore, even when people are aware that they are witnessing a criminal event, the trauma of the event and the concern for their own safety or for the safety of others may overshadow their concerns with being an accurate witness to the event.

The criminal justice system regularly struggles to resolve difficult problems of proof that often leave lingering doubts about what really happened. Although the system ordinarily does an impressive job under these circumstances,[9] in some cases our common-sense judgments are wrong. Thus, for example, each year prisoners convicted of rape based on convincing eyewitness testimony are released after years of confinement when new DNA testing provides scientific proof of their innocence.[10] These cases serve to remind us of the potential fallibility of all witnesses and the juries and judges that assess the evidence presented.

In the prosecution of old crimes, the passage of time exacerbates these normal problems of sorting out what happened. Many problems of proof in some prosecutions of old crimes are not at all complex or the subject of much debate. The effect of the passage of time on the unavailability of witnesses through death, disability, or disappearance and the loss or destruction of physical evidence are some of the obvious limitations on reaching accurate results in some long-delayed prosecutions. "Evidence is, by its nature, fragile and susceptible to destruction over time, as memories fade and witnesses die or become otherwise unavailable."[11] As seen in the *Grandjambe* case discussed in chapter 4, in which two of the witnesses needed by the defense had died by the time that the prosecution was instituted 40 years after the crime,[12] the loss or destruction of evidence may affect all parties. Because the state bears the burden of proving the elements of the crime charged, however, the unavailability of evidence ordinarily has a disproportionate impact on the prosecution. Prosecutors accordingly are often wary of retrying cases that have been reversed on appeal many years after the original conviction. Defense lawyers have often used delay to their advantage.[13]

The longer the delay between the crime and its prosecution, the greater the likelihood that some critical evidence will be lost. Ordinary crimes not solved and prosecuted in a timely fashion, such as the sales of illegal drugs and home burglaries, are not often prosecuted in a delayed manner. Instead, the unresolved crimes that are more likely to continue to demand our attention and law enforcement resources long after their occurrence are extraordinary crimes distinguished by their horror or magnitude: murder, child sexual abuse, and war crimes. The effect of the passage of time on memory in the prosecution of these extraordinary crimes is less clear. Whatever normal forgetting does to our memories of ordinary events, we may reasonably wonder about its effect on our memories of extraordinary events.

First, we might wonder about the difference in the formation of memories of extraordinary or salient events, such as war crimes or child sexual abuse, as contrasted with memories of more typical, less salient events. Are perceptions of extraordinary, horrific events so likely to be indelibly etched in our memories that we should give special weight to the testimony of witnesses to these events, or are memories of these events subject to the same frailties afflicting memories of ordinary events? If the latter is true, then we should be equally cautious in assessing the testimony of witnesses who recount both horrific and nonhorrific events that occurred decades ago.

Second, because of their salience, we might wonder about the availability of memories of these events. Because the events that are the subject of delayed prosecution are often so horrific, should we expect people who have perceived them to be consumed daily by these memories, and thus be suspicious of the testimony of witnesses who have not continuously remembered the horrific events? Alternatively, should we expect people who have often perceived horrific events to seek refuge from them, and thus conclude that continuously remembering these events is not necessarily a hallmark of accurate memories of horrific events?

To understand the problems that the passage of time and the salience of these events play on memory in accurately determining old crimes requires an examination of the process of remembering. Fortunately, there is a large body of research examining the way we remember. Perhaps the most important lesson to be learned from this research is that memory does not work like a camera that reproduces and stores images capable of being reliably recalled at our pleasure, if only we have the right cue or prompt. Although people's daily lives provide evidence that in the main, the broad contours of memory ordinarily work well enough to get them to their jobs each day and home each night, memories are not simply accurate facsimiles of external reality.[14] At times, human memory output substantially differs from human memory input.[15]

Our memory of an event is not simply a retrieved original sensory image. The memory process is constructive, not reproductive.[16] The information we remember is determined by a complex series of activities from the time we are exposed to information until we later try to recall it.[17] The main stages of the memory process are the encoding, storage, and retrieval of information.

Encoding is the process of registering information in memory. Only information that is encoded can be stored for later retrieval.[18] Because we cannot give equal attention to everything going on around us, however, we do not encode everything that we experience. People have a limited capacity for how much information they can take in, and they selectively encode some information at the cost of not encoding other information. Thus, for example, the more people who were present at an event and the less time that the witness had to observe the event, the more cautious we should be about the accuracy of the witness' identification of people associated with that event.

In addition to our attention capacity, what we encode and how well we encode it is affected by a number of other considerations. The amount of prior knowledge a person has about an event affects the ability to develop a schema or framework to encode it.[19] For example, we would expect to encode more accurate information about a conversation in our own language than in an unfamiliar foreign or technical language. The interest value or salience of an event to a person affects the likelihood that it will be encoded. We pay more attention to events that we regard as important to us or to actors or events that stand out to us. For example, a man is more likely to pay attention to a report of the results of a sporting event that he follows than one that he has never played or followed. The duration and repetition of the original event affects the likelihood that it will be encoded. Good teachers, for example, know the importance of repeating important points. In addition, the stress level at the time of encoding the original event can have a negative effect on encoding. One study of crime victims revealed that their ability to describe the race, sex, age, height, weight, build, complexion, hair color, and eye color of their assailants was inversely related to the severity of the crime.[20] Robbery victims were able to provide more complete descriptions of their assailants than rape or assault victims, and uninjured victims were able to provide more complete descriptions of their assailants than injured victims.[21]

Critical to understanding the issues of memory involved in the prosecution of old crimes is what has been called the "flashbulb memories" of the circumstances in which someone first learned about a surprising, consequential event.[22] Whatever problems the passage of time poses for memories of ordinary events, are memories of salient events differently affected by the passage of time? Intuitively, there is great appeal to the claim that memories of surprising, special events are forever clearly and accurately frozen in memory. For example, many people have vivid memories associated with their first learning about startling events such as the assassination of President John F. Kennedy or the explosion of the Challenger space shuttle. Are memories of traumatic events of great salience more likely to be accurately and indelibly encoded, immune to subsequent distortion while stored in memory? Or are these memories subject to the same construction and decay as memories of ordinary, everyday events? Understanding flashbulb memories may shed light on important aspects of our memories for traumatic events in the prosecution of old crimes.

Some researchers have claimed that flashbulb memories are the result of a special encoding mechanism that renders memories of emotionally arousing events accurate and indelible.[23] Recent research, however, suggests that the salience of these events narrows the way in which we perceive and subsequently encode them, and that, given their importance, these memories are often shaped by their rehearsal and retelling.[24] Studies of the memory of survivors of death camps, natural disasters, and serious accidents reveal that the survivors have often distorted important aspects of these events, including who or what caused them harm.[25] Indeed, even Brown and Kulik, who coined the term "flashbulb memories," reported that their study found that while such memories often included vivid details of an event, they were also often incomplete.[26] Moreover, particularly important in the context of prosecuting old crimes, the aging process seems to have a negative impact on the ability to retain flashbulb memories.[27]

Storage, the second phase of the memory process, first entails short-term memory store for encoded events and, subsequently, long-term storage of these events. Because of limited memory capacity, not all memories survive the short-term memory store to enter a long-term memory store. For example, even if a student received an A on a test that he or she took 10 years ago, it is unlikely that he or she could get an A on that same test today relying on the memories that he or she stored and encoded then, particularly if the subject of the test is unrelated to current interests or activities. Encoded information can be transformed, fortified, or lost during long-term memory storage.[28] The passage of time usually has an adverse effect on recall, whereas the number of times that the event has been re-experienced usually strengthens recall. When intervening experiences are congruent with the encoded experience, they may solidify the initial memory; when intervening experiences are incongruent with the encoded experience, they may interfere with the initial stored memory.[29]

For example, questioning styles that suggest a particular version of an event may shape the memory of the event in long-term storage. Thus, suggestive questioning about an event may transform its encoding to reflect the suggestion about what occurred. For example, in one study witnesses questioned about a film of a car crash gave higher estimates when asked about the speed of the cars when they "smashed" than when asked about the speed of the cars when they "bumped."[30] In addition, although the film depicted no broken glass, those asked about the collision with a question using the word "smashed" were more likely to recall having seen broken glass after the accident than those asked about what they observed with a question using the word "bumped."

Retrieval of stored information is the final step in the memory process. We are not necessarily able to retrieve all of the information that we have placed in long-term storage. A variety of cognitive as well as social factors influence the extent to which memories can be recalled. These include the condition of the original memory and whether it has undergone decay, the cues that the interviewer gives, the extent to which an event conforms to our expectations and beliefs about the event, and the desire of the individual to retrieve the old memory.[31] For example, one study comparing the memories of survivors of Camp Erika, a Nazi concentration camp, a few years after their release with their memories 40 years later revealed remarkable consistency about camp conditions and daily routines. However, 40 years later many survivors could not recall the names of fellow prisoners and guards.[32]

This finding is consistent with studies that examine how the aging process affects the ability to make accurate identifications. Eyewitness studies reveal that the likelihood of false (erroneous) identifications increases in elderly witnesses.[33] One theory offered to explain this increase in false identifications is that the strategy that elderly adults use to make identifications, comparing the face to be identified with known faces, increases the risk of mistaken identifications when the face to be identified is subjectively familiar.

Differences in Memory in Adults and Children

Some prosecutions of old crimes entail the testimony of adults who claim to have witnessed relevant events as children. In those child sexual abuse cases in which the complainant claims to have repressed memories of the abuse for many years but the memories were only recently recovered as an adult, we are confronted with memories of events encoded and stored as a child and sought to be retrieved as an adult. The prosecution of war crimes, particularly in cases in which the only living survivors were children when the crimes were committed, also necessarily involves memories of events encoded and stored as a child, sought to be retrieved as an adult. It is therefore important to understand what differences, if any, there are in the encoding and storage of these childhood memories and their retrieval when the witness is an adult.

Children encode, store, and retrieve memories in much the same way as adults.[34]

The critical differences in assessing memories encoded and stored as a child are the ability of children to understand the events they witness and their vulnerability to adult suggestion. Subject to decay or forgetting, the memories of children who understand what they witness and who have not been subject to adult suggestion are, as a class, no more or less reliable than adult-encoded memories.[35]

To encode information for later storage and retrieval, children, like adults, require an interpretive framework for understanding an event. In normal development, our interpretive frameworks for understanding events improve as we get older. For example, recognizing this aspect of development, most parents talk to their children about appropriate playground behavior long before they discuss human sexuality with them. Thus, when we seek the memories of a child witness, it is necessary to determine whether, given age and experience, the child witness had developed an interpretive framework for understanding the legally relevant events. In the absence of contamination by suggestion, children recall information about as accurately as adults if they have a framework for comprehending the events or if the events are familiar to them.[36]

Children possess impressive memory capacity, but very young children have not yet acquired a complete framework for understanding their personal experience of the world around them. Although a very young child may observe and store an experience, the absence of contextual cues affects the child's capacity to retrieve those memories.[37] In addition, the "social context and the extent to which adults can help children structure their experiences . . . may account for individual differences in memories for early childhood trauma."[38] Thus, it is not likely that adults can gain access to verbal memories before the age of 2.[39] However, people may have memory of salient personal events from an earlier age than previously thought. They may recall from as early as age 2 being hospitalized or the birth of a sibling, whereas as early as age 3 they may remember the death of a family member or a family move.[40] Thus, attempts to prosecute old crimes, such as child sexual abuse, based on witness memories of events that occurred before age 2 should be viewed with great suspicion, and the methods through which these memories were recalled should be subject to careful scrutiny, taking into account such factors as the child's cognitive development and social support.

Given the stakes and the interests of the various participants in the criminal justice system, the effect of suggestion on adult and child witnesses is of paramount concern. The parties to criminal prosecutions have an interest in witnesses remembering a particular version of the relevant events and may intentionally or unintentionally suggest that version of the events to a witness. In the case of child witnesses, concerns with suggestibility are particularly acute. A host of beliefs about children's penchant for fantasy, limited memory capacity, or failure to appreciate the gravity of legal proceedings lead many to view the testimony of child witnesses with great skepticism.[41] There is also an abiding concern that even the most conscientious examiners of children will have to resort to suggestive questioning styles because children asked nonleading questions (e.g., "tell us what you did last Saturday") tend to respond quite briefly (e.g., "nothing") and are therefore unlikely to provide much legally relevant information to help determine guilt or innocence.

Although adults are also vulnerable to suggestion, within particular contexts this vulnerability is more acute in children.[42] This higher degree of vulnerability is based on an interplay among inefficient encoding,[43] the interviewer, and the style of interview questions. Several well-known prosecutions provide examples of suggestive interviewing of children that cast doubt on the accuracy of their resulting trial testimony. One well-known example of this issue was brought to public light in the McMartin Preschool Manhattan Beach sexual abuse cases. There, a combination of poor interview techniques performed by authority figures and large-scale panic yielded progressively bizarre and unbelievable stories from children alleging abuse. Those children who admitted to investigators that abuse had occurred were rewarded, whereas those children who denied that abuse had occurred were ridiculed by investigators. At the conclusion of this 2½-year trial, many of the jurors believed that some abuse had occurred, but they could not sort out which portion of the children's testimony to believe and which portion to discredit. Ultimately, as noted by the foreman of the jury, this concern with suggestion resulted in the collapse of the state's case: "If any one thing put a shadow of doubt on the whole thing, it was the interviewing techniques of therapists who questioned the children after the allegations surfaced."[44]

Another well-known example of suggestive interviewing resulted in the overturning of Margaret Kelly Michael's conviction for molesting 20 preschool children while she was a teacher's aid in Maplewood, New Jersey. The ground on which the conviction was overturned was a finding that the interviews of the victims were "coercive and unduly suggestive."[45] Ultimately, the interviewers had assumed that each child they interviewed had been abused, and they persuaded the children that they would feel better if they confirmed these assumptions, as their other helpful classmates had done. Overzealous interviewers, unfounded beliefs that children do not lie about sexual abuse, and reliance on suggestive questions led to a series of similar incidents in the 1980s.[46] These sexual abuse cases with allegations from multiple victims all revealed noteworthy difficulties with the children being suggestible.[47] Unfortunately, there is no evidence that the professional judgment of sexual abuse specialists is more capable than that of anyone else distinguishing memories induced by false suggestions from true memories.[48]

Demand characteristics, the role that an interviewer and other situational factors play in eliciting memories, are important in the case of children's memories. This effect comes into play with the child witness through the interviewers who may interact with the child. These interviewers may include police officers, social workers, teachers, judges, attorneys, and parents. Research indicates that adults asked leading questions are more subject to suggestion from authoritative sources than from nonauthoritative sources.[49] One reason that children are more likely than adults to be influenced by leading questions is that children are less authoritative than most of the individuals who surround them. Children may attempt to please authority figures by responding to suggestive requests for information with details that the children think the adults want, even if they are inaccurate.

Interview style also affects children's suggestibility. The retrieval of memory through free recall, using broad, open-ended questions such as "tell us what happened yesterday after you came home from school," appears to produce more accurate, although less complete, information in the case of children.[50] Specific questions by an interviewer using more focused questions such as "did anyone touch you anywhere" may elicit more detailed information but risk giving rise to inaccurate statements or affirmations. Leading, suggestive, and closed-ended questions that call for an affirmative or negative response increase errors in reporting events. Therefore, children are more likely to provide accurate, although less complete, information in the case of a free report with minimal influence from an interviewer.[51] If a child's information is encoded efficiently, which is difficult to assess, it will be less vulnerable to suggestion. In general, children younger than the age of 5 are likely to be more suggestible than are older children.[52]

There are some indications that if new information is introduced during the questioning period, the recollection itself can be altered. Therefore, the verbalized assumptions made by the interviewer cannot only elicit inaccurate information, but also can lead the child to encode this false information into memory. Once inaccurate memories have been created through the introduction of new material and incorporated into a child's story, there is no basis to think that the child's earlier perceptions can be disentangled from erroneous information introduced by subsequent questioning.[53]

The conclusion that children are more suggestible than adults is, however, dangerous in the abstract. There are a number of confounding and interrelated variables that should be kept in mind. In the case of normal development, a child's resistance to suggestion increases with age. Thus, for example, teenagers are generally more resistant to suggestion than preschool children. Resistance to suggestion is also positively correlated with the personal significance or centrality of the experience to the child.[54] Thus, children are generally more willing to respond to suggestions about their recollections of events that are not consequential to them than events that are consequential to them.

Recovered Memory

Another memory issue in the prosecution of old crimes relates to reports of the consistency of memories of these crimes. Whereas an adult's childhood memories of war crimes are often reported as being consistently remembered, one type of prosecution of old crimes involves claims of accurate childhood memories that were not available for a long period of time and that later became available as an adult. Claims that a person repressed memories of child sexual abuse after the event for an extended period of time and then later recovered those memories as an adult requires that we ask whether there is a good reason to expect that accurate childhood memories of traumatic events can be submerged, only to emerge intact later in life. There are two distinct views on this question.[55] Unfortunately, where one begins this inquiry often seems to determine where one comes out; the professional camps have achieved little common ground in their discussion, save to agree that suggestive questioning and similar memory work designed to find abuse is dangerous and misguided. The two camps are represented by the experimental psychologists and the treating clinicians and researchers.

Experimental psychologists acknowledge that child sexual abuse is a serious problem in society but question the accuracy of proving its existence through the use of recovered repressed memories. In the light of the findings of rigorous biological and social sciences research, experimental psychologists claim that there is no good evidence that accurate memories of a traumatic experiences can be submerged and then recovered years later.[56] They point out that, for most people who have experienced traumatic events, the problem is exactly the opposite—the persistence of intrusive memories of traumatic events as reflected in the diagnostic criteria for posttraumatic stress disorder.[57] These psychologists claim that the only evidence for recovered repressed memory is clinical experience, in which people, often undergoing therapy, recall a memory of a previous traumatic event,[58] and that these claims of repression and accurate recovery of intact memories are rarely independently corroborated.[59] They point out that memory is fallible and that suggestive and improper memory work (e.g., hypnotic age regression, direct suggestion, guided imagery, and body memory analysis), used by many psychotherapists who think it is common for patients to repress memories of childhood sexual abuse, may lead to the recovery of false memories.[60] Thus, although acknowledging that child sexual abuse is an extensive and significant problem, they point to substantial research indicating that memories of traumatic events do not get lost and then subsequently rediscovered.

Treating therapists and researchers who regard claims of recovered repressed-memories as credible maintain that the occurrence of memory repression is often more reliable than experimental psychologists suggest. They claim that dissociation is the most likely explanation of loss of access to, and then retrieval of, memories of severe trauma, including childhood abuse.[61] They point to the current wide acceptance of the connection among severe childhood trauma; adult dissociative disorders; and problems in the encoding, storage, and retrieval of memories. To cope with an overwhelming trauma like child sexual abuse, they maintain that a child must develop a defensive strategy, such as dissociation and numbing, that can interfere with the normal memory processes. They suggest that something in the current environment, a retrieval cue or trigger of some sort, may reduce the use of numbing strategies, thereby allowing for access to or recovery of these stored memories. The reduction of numbing may be gradual or abrupt, but in either case it may improve the recall of previously weak memory traces, including the event of childhood sexual abuse.

Those who are prepared to believe repressed-memory claims note that although inappropriate suggestive memory work may result in the occurrence of some false memories, that does not rule out the validity of all recovered memories.[62] Therefore, they contend that "memory experts" should not automatically attribute claims of recovered memories to suggestion on the part of the therapist but instead should treat them as a frequent concomitant of psychotherapy.[63]

What then does this research mean for the prospect of accuracy in the prosecution of old crimes? Although the salience of these events may cause us to pay closer attention to them, thereby increasing the likelihood that we encode them, their salience provides no assurance that we have accurately encoded them or that we can later recall these events untouched by the normal process of memory decay, distortion, or transformation. Memories of salient events, like memories of ordinary events, are constructive rather than reproductive.

What does the research say about the effect of the salience of these events, which are the subject of the prosecution of old crimes, on the availability of memories of these events? Although there is yet an unresolved division among mental health experts about recovered repressed-memory claims, there is general consensus that most individuals who experience childhood trauma such as sexual abuse consistently remember all or some part of that trauma.[64] In addition, there is now agreement that certain therapeutic practices are particularly troubling. For example, there are fewer concerns with memories of trauma that arise spontaneously than with those that arise as the result of memory-recovery techniques.[65] We should subject to heightened legal scrutiny memories recovered after a therapist told a patient who had bulimia nervosa, and who initially reported no childhood sexual abuse, that bulimia is a symptom of repressed memories of childhood sexual abuse, that the failure to remember is common to child sexual abuse survivors, and that healing depends on remembering the incidents of abuse. In addition, the use of memory-recovery techniques, such as hypnosis, age regression, guided imagery, sodium amytal, and instructions to work at remembering the child sexual abuse, should be carefully scrutinized.

These concerns with memory for salient events and suggestibility are not, of course, limited to child sexual abuse. One case involving the prosecution of old crimes that dramatically reflects these concerns involves John Demjanjuk. Demjanjuk, a factory worker in Cleveland, Ohio, was identified in 1976 as Ivan the Terrible, the sadistic executioner who was one of the operators of the diesel engine that manufactured the gas for the gas chamber in the Nazi death camp near Treblinka, Poland, in which over 850,000 Jews were murdered.[66] Treblinka was not a work camp; its sole purpose was to kill Jews. Within these horrific environs, Ivan the Terrible gained his nickname by his unusually cruel treatment of his victims. The only survivors of Treblinka were the approximately 50 Jews who escaped the camp in an uprising shortly before the remainder of the Jews held there were killed. These survivors had been in close proximity to Ivan and the other guards for a year at Treblinka. When the U.S. investigation targeting Demjanjuk got underway several decades later, the surviving escapees were presented with a photographic array containing a 1951 photo of Demjanjuk taken when he emigrated to the United States (there was no available picture of him in 1942–1943 when he was alleged to have worked at Treblinka). Five of the surviving escapees positively identified the photograph of Demjanjuk as the man they knew as Ivan the Terrible. Based on their testimony, Demjanjuk was found to have misrepresented his wartime activities and whereabouts when he applied for entry into the United States and subsequently on his application for citizenship. He was then denaturalized and extradited to Israel where he was tried, convicted, and sentenced to death for war crimes at Treblinka. Subsequently, in a decision that shocked the world, the Israel Supreme Court reversed Demjanjuk's conviction and entered an acquittal based on statements of Ukrainian guards at Treblinka who identified another man, Ivan Marchenko, as Ivan the Terrible.[67] Demjanjuk's denaturalization was then reopened by the U.S. Circuit Court of Appeals for governmental misconduct in failing to turn over exculpatory information to Demjanjuk's attorneys.[68] Demjanjuk's citizenship was restored accompanied by a finding that Department of Justice lawyers had acted "with reckless disregard for their duty to the court."[69]

The *Demjanjuk* case is chilling because of the horror of the crime charged, the certainty of the identifications made by the Holocaust survivors who labored in close proximity to Ivan the Terrible 3 decades earlier, and the Ukrainian guards' testimony that Ivan the Terrible was someone other than Demjanjuk. The investigation of Demjanjuk is rife with suggestive questioning and the dismissal of exculpatory evidence. If we encounter such problems in cases of this import, where the world is watching and we might expect the criminal justice system to marshal its best investigatory efforts, what can we hope for in the more mundane prosecutions of old crimes where there is little public accounting?

Challenges for the Justice System

The prosecution of old crimes presents special challenges for the criminal justice system. In itself, the passage of time in the prosecution of old crimes exacerbates the problem, present in all cases, of ascertaining the truth. Evidence is perishable, and with the passage of significant time, both physical and testimonial evidence are inherently less available. Thus, the prosecution of old crimes often presents prosecutors with special investigatory challenges.

Crimes that are prosecuted a significant time after the event are unique; they may be particularly heinous like the 1969 rape and murder of 8-year-old Susan Nason, particularly notorious like the 1962 Great Train Robbery, or particularly chilling like the prosecutions of former German army officer Erich Priebke for the 1944 execution of 335 Italian civilians. Ordinary crimes that are not successfully investigated in a timely manner are less likely to survive the bar of the statute of limitations (see chap. 4). They are also less likely to command significant investigatory resources and, therefore, less likely to be prosecuted after many years. Thus, the cases that are prosecuted a considerable time after the crime tend to be those in which society claims a special stake in bringing the defendant to justice.

Relying on inherently perishable proof in the prosecution of these crimes does not mean that justice cannot be done. Instead, it means that we must proceed with great care. Because of the nature of the crimes at issue, we have a duty to see that the criminal justice system does not forget these cases. Because of the nature of the problems of proof in these cases, we have a duty to see that their investigation and proof meets the most rigorous scientific and evidentiary standards. Justice demands that we zealously pursue both of these goals.

Endnotes

1. Blaise Pascal, *Thoughts,* trans. W. F. Trotter. Brunschvicg 395 Lafum 406 (New York: Collier & Sons, 1936).
2. See chapter 2.
3. *Id.*
4. See chapter 7.
5. See, e.g., *United States v. Beechum,* 582 F.2d 898, 908 (5th cir. 1978): "Truth is the essential objective of our adversary system of justice." *See* Craig M. Bradley and Joseph L. Hoffmann, "Public perception, justice, and the 'search for truth' in criminal cases," *Southern California Law Review* 69 (1996):1267–1302, at 1270.
6. Michael L. Radelet, Hugo Adam Bedau, and Constance E. Putnam, *In spite of innocence: Erroneous convictions in capital cases* (Boston: Northeastern University Press, 1992).
7. *In re Winship,* 397 U.S. 358, 362–363 (1970): "The reasonable-doubt standard plays a vital role in the American scheme of criminal procedure. It is a prime instrument for reducing the risk of convictions resting on factual error. The standard provides concrete substance for the presumption of innocence—that bedrock 'axiomatic and elementary' principle whose 'enforcement lies at the foundation of the administration of our criminal law.' "
8. James Bradley Thayer, *A preliminary treatise on evidence at the common law* (Boston: Little, Brown, 1898).
9. See Daniel Shuman et al., "Jury service—It may change your mind: Perceptions of

fairness of jurors and nonjurors," *Southern Methodist University Law Review* 46 (1992): 449–479 (describing how jurors' experiences enhanced their perceptions of the fairness of the criminal justice system).

10. Lisa W. Foderado, "DNA frees convicted rapist after nine years," *New York Times,* July 31, 1991, at B1; Laura Frank and John Hanchette, "GNS special report: Cases that have hinged on DNA evidence," *Gannett News Service,* July 1, 1994 (available in 1994 WL 11250611); J. Michael Kennedy, "DNA test clears man convicted of rape counts," *Los Angeles Times,* Jan. 16, 1994, at B1 (available in 1994 WL 2125161); Larry King, "Salvaged by science: DNA helps set the innocent free," *New Orleans Times-Picayune,* May 14, 1995, at A22; "Man cleared of rapes after four years in prison," *Washington Times,* May 3, 1992, at A2; "Man convicted on false testimony in '90 rape freed," *Dallas Morning News,* July 13, 1994, at 12D (available in 1994 WL 6084243); Janet Williams, "Man freed after serving eight years for rape he didn't commit," *Indianapolis Star,* Dec. 18, 1993, at A1 (reporting the case of Dwayne Scruggs of IN).

11. *Thigpen v. Smith,* 792 F.2d 1507, 1514 (11th Cir. 1986).

12. *Regina v. Grandjambe,* 108 C.C.C. (3d 1996).

13. See, e.g., Stacey Zolt, "Weston attorneys appeal decision on mental exam," *Roll Call,* Feb. 4, 1999: "Erik Christian, assistant U.S. Attorney, opened the discussions on behalf of the government. 'From the very outset of this case,' he said, 'it has been marked by delay, delay, delay, delay.' Christian said the government is aggravated by what it perceives to be deliberate slowdowns by the defense team. In the defense response to the judge, Boss said, 'both Mr. Kramer and myself are troubled by the suggestion that we're involved in an attempt to delay.' "

14. Gerald D. Fischbach and Joseph T. Coyle, *Preface x: Memory distortion: How minds, brains and societies reconstruct the past,* Daniel L. Schacter, Ed. (Cambridge, MA: Harvard University Press, 1995).

15. Daniel L. Schacter, "Memory distortion: History and current status." In *Memory distortion: How minds, brains and societies reconstruct the past,* Daniel L. Schacter, Ed. (Cambridge, MA: Harvard University Press, 1995).

16. Frederic C. Bartlett, *Remembering: A study in experimental and social psychology* (Cambridge, MA: Cambridge University Press, 1932).

17. Stephen Ceci and Maggie Bruck, *Jeopardy in the courtroom: A scientific analysis of children's testimony* (Washington, DC: American Psychological Association, 1995).

18. *Id.*

19. *Id.*

20. L. L. Keuhn, "Looking down a gun barrel: Perception and violent crime," *Perceptual and Motor Skills* 39 (1974):1159–1164.

21. *Id.* at 1161.

22. Roger Brown and James Kulik, "Flashbulb memories," *Cognition* 5 (1977):73–99.

23. Lenore Terr, "What happens to early memories of trauma? A study of 20 children under age five at the time of documented traumatic events," *Journal of the American Academy of Child and Adolescent Psychiatry* 27 (1988): 96–104.

24. Gillian Cohen, Martin A. Conway, and Elizabeth A. Maylor, "Flashbulb memories in older adults," *Psychology and Aging* 9 (1994):454–463.

25. *Id.* at 193.

26. Roger Brown and James Kulik, "Flashbulb memories," *Cognition* 5 (1977):73–99.

27. Cohen et al., "Flashbulb memories."

28. Charles C. Brainerd et al., "The development of forgetting and reminiscence," *Monographs of the Society for Research on Child Development* 55 (1990):3–4(Serial No. 222).

29. Ceci and Bruck, *Jeopardy in the courtroom,* at 42.

30. Elizabeth F. Loftus and John C. Palmer, "Reconstruction of automobile deconstruction: An example of the interaction between language and memory." In *Readings in social*

psychology: The art and science of research, Steven Fein and Steven Spencer, Eds. (Boston: Houghton Mifflin, 1996) at 143–147.

31. Ceci and Bruck, *Jeopardy in the courtroom.*

32. Willem A. Wagenaar and Jop Groeneweg, "The memory of concentration camp survivors," *Journal of Applied Cognitive Psychology* 4 (1990):77–87.

33. Douglas J. Narby, Brian L. Cutler, and Steven D. Penrod, "The effects of witness, target, and situational factors on eyewitness identifications." In *Mistaken identifications: The eyewitness, psychology, and law,* Brian L. Cutler and Steven D. Penrod, Eds. (New York: Cambridge University Press, 1995) at 23–52.

34. Marie DeLipsey and Daniel W. Shuman, *The child witness in forensic psychology for the journeyman clinician* (Austin: Texas Psychological Foundation, 1991).

35. *Id.*

36. Gail Goodman, "Picture memory: How the action schema affects retention," *Cognitive Psychology* 12 (1982): 473; D. F. Bjorkland and H. D. Hock, "Age differences in the temporal locus of memory organization in children's recall," *Journal of Experimental Child Psychology* 33 (1982): 347.

37. Robyn Fivush and Nina R. Hammond, "Autobiographical memory across the preschool years: Toward reconceptualizing childhood amnesia." In *Knowing and remembering in young children*, R. Fivush and J. A. Hudson, Eds. (New York: Cambridge University Press, 1990) at 223–248.

38. Amina Memon and Mark Young, "Desperately seeking evidence: The recovered memory debate," *Legal and Criminological Psychology* 2 (1997):1–24.

39. Elizabeth Loftus, "The reality of repressed memories," *American Psychologist* 48 (1993): 518–537.

40. JoNell A. Usher and Ulric Neisser, "Childhood amnesia and the beginnings of memory for four early life events," *Journal of Experimental Psychology* 122 (1993):155–165.

41. Judy Cashmere and Kay Bussey, "Judicial perceptions of child witness competence," *Law and Human Behavior* 20 (1996):313–334.

42. Ronald L. Cohen and Mary Anne Harnick, "The susceptibility of the child witness to suggestion," *Law and Human Behavior* 4 (1980):201–210; Philip Dale et al., "The influence of the form of the question on the eyewitness testimony of preschool children," *Journal of Psycholinguistic Research* 7 (1978):269–277; Gail S. Goodman and Rebecca S. Reed, "Age differences in eyewitness testimony," *Law and Human Behavior* 10 (1986):317–332.

43. D. F. Bjorkland and H. S. Hock, "Age differences in temporal locus of memory organization in children's recall," *Journal of Experimental Psychology* 33 (1982):347–362.

44. Michael C. Tippery, "McMartin jury deadlocked—Mistrial declared," *UPI,* July 27, 1990 (LEXIS–NEXIS Library, Wires File).

45. *State v. Michaels,* 642 A.2d 1372, 1380 (N.J. 1994).

46. John E. B. Myers, "New era of skepticism regarding children's credibility," *Psychology, Public Policy, and Law* 1 (1995):387–398.

47. Debra C. Moss, "Are the children lying?" *American Bar Association Journal* 60 (1987): 31–34.

48. Stephen J. Ceci et al., "The possible role of source misattributions in the creation of false beliefs among preschoolers," *International Journal of Clinical and Experimental Hypnosis* 42 (1994):304–320.

49. M. Shantz, "Communication." In *Handbook of child psychology*, J. H. Flavell and E. M. Markman, Eds. (New York: Wiley, 1983) at 841–889.

50. Ceci and Bruck, *Jeopardy in the courtroom*, at 52–61.

51. Stephen J. Ceci et al., "Suggestibility of children's memory: Psychological implications," *Journal of Experimental Psychology* 116 (1987):38–49; Elizabeth F. Loftus, "The malleability of human memory," *American Scientist* 67 (1979):312–320.

52. Mary De Young, "A conceptual model for judging the truthfulness of a young child's allegations of sexual abuse," *American Journal of Orthopsychiatry* 56(4) (1986):476–480.

53. Ronald L. Cohen and Mary Anne Harnick, "The susceptibility of the child witness to suggestion," *Law and Human Behavior* 4 (1980):201–210; Philip Dale et al. "The influence of the form of the question on the eyewitness testimony of preschool children," *Journal of Psycholinguistic Research* 7 (1978):269–277; Gail S. Goodman and Rebecca S. Reed, "Age differences in eyewitness testimony," *Law and Human Behavior* 10 (1986):317–332.

54. Gail S. Goodman, "The child witness: Conclusions and future directions for research and legal practice," *Journal of Social Issues* 40(2) (1984):157–175; Elizabeth F. Loftus and Edith Green, "Warning: Even memory for faces may be contagious," *Law and Human Behavior* 8 (1980):323–334.

55. Judith Albert et al., *Final conclusions of the APA Working Group on the Investigation of Memories of Childhood Abuse* (American Psychological Association: Final Report, Working Group on Investigation of Memories of Childhood Abuse, 1996).

56. Peter A. Ornstein et al., *Reply to the Alpert, Brown & Courtois document: The science of memory and the practice of psychotherapy* (American Psychological Association: Final Report, Working Group on Investigation of Memories of Childhood Abuse, 1996).

57. American Psychiatric Association, *Diagnostic and statistical manual of mental disorders* (4th ed., Washington, DC: Author, 1994) at 309.81.

58. Gary M. Ernsdorff and Elizabeth F. Loftus, "Let sleeping memories lie? Words of caution about tolling the statute of limitations in cases of memory repression," *Journal of Criminal Law and Criminology* 84 (1993):129–174.

59. Judith Herman and Emily Schatzow, "Recovery and verification of memories of childhood sexual trauma," *Psychoanalytic Psychology* 4 (1987):1–10.

60. Debra Poole et al., "Psychotherapy and the recovery of memories of childhood sexual abuse: U.S. and British practitioners' opinions, practices, and experiences," *Journal of Consulting and Clinical Psychology* 63 (1995):426–437.

61. Judith L. Albert et al., *Symptomatic clients and memories of childhood sexual abuse: What the trauma and child sexual abuse literature tells us* (American Psychological Association: Final Report, Working Group on Investigation of Memories of Childhood Abuse, 1996).

62. John Briere, "Science versus politics in the delayed memory debate," *The Counseling Psychologist* 23 (1995):291–293.

63. Christine Courtois, "Scientist-practitioners and the delayed memory controversy: Scientific standards and the need for collaboration," *The Counseling Psychologist* 23 (1995):295–299.

64. Judith Albert et al., *Final conclusions of the APA Working Group on the Investigation of Memories of Childhood Abuse* (American Psychological Association: Final Report, Working Group on Investigation of Memories of Childhood Abuse, 1996).

65. D. Stephen Lindsay and J. Don Read, "'Memory work' and recovered memories of childhood sexual abuse: Scientific evidence and public, professional and personal issues," *Psychology, Public Policy, and Law* 1 (1995):846–908.

66. See Willem Wagenaar, *Identifying Ivan: A case study in legal psychology* (Cambridge, MA: Harvard University Press, 1988).

67. "Court in Israel clears Demjanuk of being Ivan, a Nazi criminal," *New York Times*, July 29, 1993, at A1.

68. *Demjanuk v. United States,* 10 F.3d 338 (6th Cir. 1993).

69. R. Kropko, "Demjanuk's US citizenship restored," *Associated Press Online,* Feb. 21, 1998.

Chapter 7
JUSTICE AND THERAPY:
The Role of the Law in Healing the Victim

How do crime victims feel when the person who harmed them is arrested, convicted, and punished? A commonly expressed reaction is relief. Many victims talk about the closure that results when the guilty are punished. "Now I can get on with rest of my life," the victim may say. "Justice has been done." Similar sentiments of relief or resolution are often expressed by the relatives of murder victims when they witness the conviction of the murderer. In their eyes, the conviction signals the end of a chapter, the end of a period of suffering and anxiety during which the knowledge that the perpetrator had yet to be punished had a significant effect on their ability to recover from their loss.

It would be surprising if the frequency with which these feelings are publicly expressed by crime victims did not lead to us to conclude that bringing the perpetrator to justice is an essential component of a victim's recovery. Even if forgiveness plays a integral role in the healing process, as discussed in chapter 3, this does not preclude a healing role for punishment. This, after all, is what many victims appear to be saying. Without punishing those who have wronged them, they would be unable to escape the sheer weight of the memory of what was done to them. Punishing the wrongdoer becomes an act of closure. It acknowledges the wrong, condemns the wrongdoer, and consigns the wrong to the past. Borrowing by analogy from legal doctrine, the offense is *res judicata*, something that has been dealt with and cannot be resurrected.

If we accept this view of the therapeutic role of formal criminal punishment, and if we were convinced that punishment is only visited on the guilty, even in the case of old crimes, then there is always good reason to punish old crimes, provided, of course, that a victim (however broadly defined) survives. If punishment is therapeutic for crime victims, the prosecution of the offender is not simply a requirement of formal justice; it is something that society owes to the victim as a means of assisting his or her recovery. The criminal justice system, of course, has many other objectives—protecting the public in general and reinforcing societal norms, for instance—but it certainly counts among its central aims the objective of providing some measure of consolation for those who have been wronged.

Although the interests of victims have rarely been at the forefront of the criminal justice system's concerns, it is now widely accepted that the criminal justice system should treat the victim with at least minimal decency. Hence the growing insistence on giving outcome information to the victim and, more controversially, admitting victim impact statements or allowing the victim to play a role in the determination of sentence.[1] What is apparent in these developments is a recognition that the criminal justice system should seek to minimize the extent of the victim's suffering and, incidental to this, help the victim on the road to recovery.

To link this admittedly laudable goal with an inevitable need of victims for the prosecution of all crimes, and in particular old crimes, as a requirement of healing, is to make an assumption about the therapeutic role of punishment that simply may not be justified. Even if punishment of a wrongdoer benefits society, does it benefit the victim? Although there is much anecdotal reporting that victims believe that the prosecution and punishment of the wrongdoer will make them feel better and, therefore, assist their recovery from the effect of the crime, is this really so? Crime victims may genuinely believe that they will be improved by their participation in the criminal justice process, and it may be that immediately after the trial or institution of punishment, many victims and their families accurately report satisfaction at the outcome. But this does not provide evidence that the course of recovery for the victim or the victim's family is necessarily better or different than it would have been had there not been a prosecution, nor does it tell us anything about the recovery of those crime victims who deal with their trauma outside the criminal justice system through psychotherapy, caring family and friends, or faith. Moreover, anecdotal evidence must be balanced against the reports of those crime victims whose experiences with the criminal justice system left them feeling victimized by the system that they thought was there to help them.

The victim who participates in the criminal justice process may have recovered at the same rate even if there had been no prosecution; it may even be that the recovery would have been quicker without participation in the criminal justice process. For some victims, the punishment of the wrongdoer and the process it entails may in fact be highly therapeutic, for some it may be neutral, and for others it may be harmful. The difficulty lies in generalizing or making generic claims about the causal relationship between the criminal justice process and victim recovery. Although some victims report that they feel relieved or unburdened by the operation of the criminal justice process, some report that they did not find the solace that they expected, and others report that they felt victimized yet a second time by the process. What distinguishes these responses? In particular, we might inquire as to the effect on outcome of factors such as systemic differences in the criminal justice system, such as victim-participation procedures or rules limiting the scope of victim cross-examination; individual differences in the victims, for instance, personality characteristics, familial support, or prior traumas; or the nature of the crimes to which they were subjected, for example, assault by a stranger or assault by a friend or family member.

Although the answer may be complex, the question that is at the core of this chapter is quite simple: Is justice therapeutic? In an ideal world, many want to believe, people justly reap what they deserve.[2] This notion of the world as a just place provides people with security not only because it assures that those who commit wrongs will be punished but also because it assures that those who are innocent will not. According to this view, the settlement of this accounting through the criminal justice system has a therapeutic effect for those harmed by criminal conduct by reinforcing the security and stability inherent in a just world. If reinforcing or restoring this sense of a just world is an important therapeutic aspect of recovery for crime victims, the prosecution of all crimes, particularly old crimes, is critically important for the mental and emotional health of crime victims apart from other societal concerns, such as retribution and deterrence. The precise way in which the courts might play a role in the healing process of crime victims, however, has not been carefully explored or explained. We might ask whether crime victims who see their assailants appropriately punished experience healing denied to other crime victims. If so, why, and how is the healing process altered when justice is delayed? In this chapter, we consider what psychological researchers and theorists have to offer on these questions and their implications for the psychological well-being of the victims of old crimes.

Is Justice Therapeutic?

Unfortunately, little direct study of whether justice is therapeutic has been undertaken. It might seem that there are numerous naturalistic experiments that provide the opportunity to assess the therapeutic effect of the judicial system for crime victims. However, it is easier to identify questions about the therapeutic effect of the judicial system for crime victims than it is to identify rigorous efforts to provide answers to these questions. Consider some of the naturalistic experiments that have offered the opportunity to examine these fundamental questions. Did German efforts at apology and victim restitution following the World War II leave victims of German war crimes psychologically better off than the victims of Japanese war crimes to whom equivalent efforts at apology or restitution were not made? Are the victims of the bombing of the Oklahoma City Federal Building psychologically better off following Timothy McVeigh's apprehension, trial, conviction, and death sentence? Do they now sleep more soundly or have fewer intrusive thoughts and feelings about the bombing than before his apprehension, trial, and conviction? How do Oklahoma City bombing victims and their families compare psychologically to the Pan Am Flight 103 Lockerbie bombing victims' families, whose wait for the apprehension of suspects was considerably longer?

Although these cases seem to present the opportunity to examine victims' psychological responses to crime and the role of the criminal justice system, there is no rigorous research examining them. Although questions abound, answers about the psychological effect of crime and the mediating role of the criminal justice system do not exist. Both those who claim that justice is therapeutic and those who claim that it is not too often rely on anecdotal evidence that may not represent the experience of most crime victims.

Of particular relevance for the prosecution of old crimes is the fact that we do not know what happens to victims of crimes that remain unprosecuted for many years or decades. From the point of view of the mental health care of the victim and the conduct of the judicial system, it is important to know how these victims cope with the harm that has befallen them and what happens to these coping strategies when prosecution is instituted many years later. Although it would be comforting to think that a courtroom confrontation of the assailant who committed an unspeakable crime many years ago is likely to help heal an open wound, we cannot be confident that this delayed confrontation will not have the opposite effect and undo whatever healing has occurred. There are questions here as to whether permitting the prosecution of old crimes will increase the likelihood that an essential element in a victim's recovery occurs or whether permitting such prosecution will encourage crime victims to remain frozen at an early stage of their psychological recovery, awaiting a prosecution that may never happen.

It is difficult for concerned people not to wonder about the effects that efforts at justice will have on victims. For example, we might wonder about the psychological effect on Holocaust survivors of the apprehension, conviction, and execution in 1962 of Adolf Eichmann, considered to be the primary architect of Hitler's Final Solution, 26 years after the end of World War II. There are many possibilities here. Holocaust survivors might have been comforted that justice was done, just as they might have been upset that so many who perpetrated this horror escaped justice. Memories of the Holocaust might also be expected to have been affected by Eichmann's trial and execution, but in this respect, as in others, different Holocaust survivors may have responded in different ways. We have no survey of the different responses of Holocaust survivors or examination of what accounted for these differences.

How did the family of Susan Nason, an 8-year-old girl who was raped and murdered outside of San Francisco in September 1969, with no suspect arrested for 21 years, cope with their tragic loss? How was their coping affected by Eileen Franklin-Lipsker's revelation that she witnessed her father, George Franklin, kill Nason but had no adult recollection of it until her memories were triggered by a glance from her own daughter 20 years later? How was Nason's family affected by the ensuing prosecution, conviction, its reversal on appeal for procedural errors, and the decision not to retry Franklin?[3] It is heartbreaking to imagine a family's reaction to the loss of a young child to a violent crime, but the legal roller coaster ride to which Nason's family was subjected, to no apparent avail, has all the trappings of a diabolical psychological torture.

Prosecutors exercise discretion whether to pursue cases. In this decision, they take into account not only the likelihood of success but also a range of other consequences, including victim-oriented considerations.[4] The question of whether it is wise to force a victim to testify or whether justice demands prosecution may properly play a role in the exercise of prosecutorial discretion in a particular case. This discretion ought to be no less thoughtfully exercised in the prosecution of old crimes, and, arguably, given the plight of the victims of crimes subject to delayed prosecution, this discretion should be even more carefully exercised in these cases. Whatever old crimes the criminal law permits the state to prosecute within the applicable statute of limitations,[5] these crimes ought to be approached with due regard for the therapeutic consequences for the victims and their families.

Although there was once a belief that crime induced psychological problems only in those victims who had preexisting mental health problems, the available research does not support that belief. There is now ample evidence that crime victims may suffer deep psychological scars that manifest themselves in such problems as anxiety and depressive disorders, drug and alcohol abuse, and sleep disorders, and that the severity of these psychological scars is often related to the degree of violence or injury involved in the crime.[6] Some crime victims experience short-term psychological problems, whereas others experience long-term problems; some victims' lives are only marginally affected by their victim experiences, and others are fundamentally altered by these experiences. Although not all victims respond to similar crimes in similar fashion, there is little doubt that crime plays a causal role in a wide variety of psychological problems.[7]

Crime victims often demand justice and express satisfaction at the conclusion of a trial when they think that justice has been achieved. During the lifetime of the East German state, many people experienced a range of suffering. Escapees to the West were shot, and dissenters suffered extensive political imprisonment. The survivors of this system proved keen to pursue the perpetrators of these wrongs, claim-ing, "It's not about revenge, it's about justice."[8] The families of the Pan Am Flight 103 Lockerbie victims similarly maintained that, when those responsible for the bombing are brought to trial, "the suffering of the families of the (victims of) the tragic incident would end too."[9] Support groups organized to assist the victims of human rights abuses during the "dirty wars" in South America and the struggle against apartheid in South Africa demand acknowledgment of past wrongs, revelation about the truth of these wrongs, and that the perpetrators be brought to justice.[10]

These efforts suggest that the trial and punishment of offenders will inevitably bring relief, but although the news reports are strewn with selected crime victims' reports of glee or frustration about criminal investigations and prosecutions, little attempt has been made to study victims' psychological responses systemically or to learn about the long-term effects of these events. After the spotlight fades and the reporters have moved on to the next story, the victims have to get on with their lives, and we know little about the effect on these lives of the prosecution of their assailant. For example, the Department of Justice's National Crime Victim Survey reports that most sexual assault victims do not report these crimes to the police,[11] yet we know little of the long-term psychological reactions of either those victims who do or do not report. Nor do we know how sexual assault victims who pursue counseling alone compare psychologically with sexual assault victims who pursue the criminal justice system alone. We are also unsure how sexual assault victims respond to convictions and acquittals of their assailants or how they react to different sets of procedural rules for the prosecution of these cases. There is no research linking conviction or harsh punishment with the victim's recovery.[12]

The few studies that address the psychology of crime victims raise more ques-tions than they answer. For example, one survey found that women who were willing to prosecute a sexual assault had higher self-esteem than those who were not.[13] Another study looking at the adjustment of rape victims found the best predictor of depression and anxiety following the rape was their psychological functioning before the rape.[14] Thus, even if researchers were to find a difference in the mental health of sexual assault victims who successfully prosecute their assailants, it would be necessary to determine whether that difference was a measure of sexual assault vic-tims' prior mental health that affects their decision to prosecute, rather than a measure of anything therapeutic about just prosecutions. Moreover, for crimes such as sexual assault, criminal prosecution may be therapeutic because the institution of a criminal prosecution may require seeking help at a hospital emergency room, which itself precipitates offers of mental health care and support, and not necessarily because of anything therapeutic within the criminal justice system.

Because of the absence of research examining the psychological effects of crim-inal prosecution on victims' recovery, many of the insights into the therapeutic effects of the justice system on victims are necessarily based on inferences drawn from related research. One theoretical explanation for the psychological effects of victim-ization is that the criminal act results in a feeling of inequity or loss of security.[15] A number of social sciences theories conceive of wrongs as creating imbalances in power that the legal system may help restore and thereby aid in the healing process. This is a concept that as seen finds its echo in philosophical theories of retribution.[16] These theories, which include equity and feminist theories, propose that "one of the key factors in healing illness is mobilizing resources of power—typically by enhancing the individual's sense of personal empowerment (from external or internal sources)."[17] They are grounded in the developing medical and social psychological literature that addresses the relationship between power and domination and between illness and disease.[18] Each theory proposes a different etiology of disempowerment. What is common to these theories, however, is that healing entails empowerment. If healing does entail empowerment, and if the successful prosecution of an assailant empowers the victim and helps the victim regain a sense of control over his or her life, justice may indeed be therapeutic for crime victims. However, research is needed to confirm or refute these theories to explain the therapeutic consequences of the operation of the criminal justice system.

Equity theory in social psychology explains harm as the result of an inequity that occurs in a relationship.[19] It defines an equitable relationship between two people as one in which one person's outcome:input ratio equals the other person's outcome: input ratio. According to equity theory, harm occurs when one person engages in an act that results in an inequitable relationship or distribution of harm, a perception of unfairness or injustice in the relationship. When people perceive a loss that is disproportionate to their perception of their responsibility for its causation, they experience an "aversive emotional state."[20] By formally reorienting the moral compass of responsibility, the criminal justice system may help adjust the imbalance caused by the criminal act. Glanville Williams's observations reflect the psychological account balance to which criminal prosecution may respond: "A person who has been wronged feels resentment, and society sympathetically identifies itself with the victim. The resentment of the victim and of society can be appeased by punishment (the criminal sanction) or satisfied by reparation (the civil sanction)."[21]

Another relevant empowerment theory is feminist theory, which contends that male-dominated institutions operate to disempower women. Feminist theorists view gender and power as inextricably linked in our society.[22] Proceeding from this premise, feminists view readjustment of this imbalance as the key to women's physical and emotional health and well-being. One attempt to apply this theory to benefit victims involves the use of tort actions for victims of rape, which may empower the rape victim.[23] By taking their recovery into their own hands, women who have been raped who disidentify themselves with stereotypical victim roles may recover more effectively and may protect themselves from future victimization by refusing to assume passive and dependent victim roles. In repudiating her assailant's power to silence her through shame, guilt, and fear, the rape victim who launches a civil suit may reject her attacker's dominance and reassert her right to self-determination and sexual autonomy.[24] Similarly, the criminal prosecution of rapists may help empower the complainant, reject the role of victim, and assert her power and control over her sexual autonomy. The criminal trial may also restore the victim's confidence in her community while providing it with the opportunity to acknowledge its respect for the victim.[25]

The psychological problems reported by many people who have been sexually abused as a child provides another context for analysis of the feminist approach to the use of the judicial system to reshape the power imbalance in relationships. Child sexual abuse victims frequently report symptoms of depression, anxiety, sexual dysfunction, self-destructive behavior, and revictimization,[26] which have been linked to "a profound sense of powerlessness engendered in victims of sexual abuse."[27] Some therapists advocate the use of the judicial system by victims of child sexual abuse as an important tool in their healing because of its empowerment potential. "When children are able to bring the abuse to an end effectively, or at least exert some control over its occurrence, they may feel less disempowered."[28] Thus, the criminal justice system may be therapeutic for victims of child sexual abuse by providing them with some control over their lives.

There is evidence, however, that whatever its therapeutic potential, child victims who testify against their abusers are at greater risk of experiencing serious mental or emotional problems than child victims who do not participate in the criminal justice system. For example, in one study tracking child sexual abuse victims, children involved in criminal court proceedings had no more than an 8% chance of matching the psychological improvement of child sexual abuse victims not involved in court proceeding.[29] Even in one of the most sophisticated studies comparing the short-term effect on testifying and nontestifying for victims of child sexual abuse and the protective factors that may assist them, such as closed-circuit television and videotaped testimony, repeated exposure to the judicial system consistently emerged as a stressor with negative effects for children and not as a therapeutic salve.[30] The more times a child testified, the greater the likelihood of it having negative effects. Thus, the therapeutic potential of the criminal justice system must be carefully measured against its practical realization.

One therapeutic technique recently used in the treatment of survivors of state-sponsored violence is "testimony psychotherapy,"[31] which entails telling and documenting the story of the survivor's trauma. It is thought to work by transforming individual narratives into a collective understanding of the experience that is then used to communicate and teach others about it. Although there is only limited controlled research examining testimony psychotherapy, that research provides "some evidence to support the claim that telling the trauma story through testimony psychotherapy can reduce symptoms and improve survivors' psychosocial functioning."[32] If testimony psychotherapy is an effective treatment for trauma survivors, it raises two legal concerns: Is it still necessary or appropriate to consider the therapeutic benefits of legal proceedings? If it is, what do the lessons of testimony psychotherapy offer for judicial testimony?

Even if testimony psychotherapy is an effective tool in treating some trauma survivors, it is still necessary to consider the therapeutic consequences of judicial testimony. For victims who have a choice, it is important to learn which is more effective. Also, because victims often do not have a choice whether to institute criminal proceedings and to testify about events that they have witnessed, it is important to learn whether the benefits of testimony psychotherapy may also exist in judicial testimony.

If testimony psychotherapy is therapeutic for survivors, does that suggest that testimony in a judicial proceeding is also likely to be therapeutic? There is good reason to be cautious. Judicial testimony and testimony psychotherapy may share little more than a label. To achieve its therapeutic potential, testimony psychotherapy requires that the survivor and interviewer establish an alliance based on sharing a common beneficent goal, that the interviewer provide a supportive environment, and that the interviewer await the survivor's readiness to tell his or her story.[33] Neither the role of the judge nor the prosecutor, and certainly not the role of the defense attorney, permit the formation of a beneficent alliance with the trauma survivor. The judicial system's agenda is to obtain relevant information from the survivor, not to permit the survivor to tell his or her story, when ready, in a therapeutic manner. At times, providing that relevant information may be therapeutic to a trauma survivor; at times it may not be therapeutic. Although courts are empowered to protect witnesses from questions that are solely intended to harass or embarrass them,[34] questions that call for relevant information but that also happen to be traumatic are not, on that basis, improper. Unlike testimony psychotherapy that proceeds according to the survivor's psychological requirements, judicial testimony proceeds according to the court's requirements. Thus, although judicial testimony has the potential to replicate the therapeutic benefits of testimony psychotherapy by permitting the survivor to tell his or her story in an important public forum, whether it will achieve therapeutic benefits in any given case seems serendipitous.

Is Delayed Justice Therapeutic?

These speculations about the therapeutic effect of the criminal justice system have been limited to the consequences of timely prosecutions. Whatever therapeutic consequences timely prosecution may have for crime victims, the effect of delayed prosecutions could be quite different. If timely prosecution is therapeutic, do delayed prosecutions confer the same therapeutic benefits as timely prosecutions, if only in a delayed manner, to victims whose recovery ultimately necessitates successful prosecution? We should consider whether delayed prosecutions risk disturbing coping mechanisms that crime victims develop for dealing with their harm. It is also possible that delayed prosecutions risk encouraging crime victims to delay their psychological recovery in anticipation of a future prosecution, much like secondary-gain theorists claim that tort litigation encourages claimants to delay their recovery until their claim is resolved.[35] Unfortunately, there is even less information available about the therapeutic consequences of delayed prosecution than timely prosecution. Thus, predicting the therapeutic consequences of delayed prosecutions requires extrapolation from theories that address timely prosecution and speculation about the effects of the passage of time.

It is certainly possible that successful prosecution is a crucial step in the healing process for all crime victims, that in its absence all crime victims cannot move on in their recovery, and that whenever this prosecution occurs it provides the same crucial benefits, albeit delayed. It is also possible that successful criminal prosecution is not a crucial step in the healing process for all victims, that in its absence many crime victims do in fact move on in their recovery, or that the therapeutic benefits of successful prosecution are enjoyed only in the case of timely prosecution. Unfortunately, at present, the evidence for both sets of theories is largely anecdotal. Some crime victims appear to recover only after successful criminal prosecution, and some appear to recover in the absence of successful prosecution or do not appear to recover even after successful prosecution.[36] Some crime victims do not appear to recover until a delayed prosecution of an old crime,[37] whereas some who had appeared to recover seemed debilitated by the delayed prosecution.[38] Perhaps the only conclusion that can fairly be drawn from the existing evidence is that recovery is a personal search for meaning that is the result of a complex interaction of a number of variables and that to assess the effects for the victim of the interaction of the crime, the criminal, the crime victim, and the criminal justice system requires rigorous study.

In the absence of that study, we are left to extrapolate from related areas of research.

One body of research that may shed light on the therapeutic value of delayed prosecution (as contrasted with no prosecution) relates to studies of the behavior of victims of sexual assault. Although there is no single way in which victims behave or respond to their assault, there is evidence that one symptom that many experience is a fear of retaliation or another sexual assault.[39] In some victims, this fear may become a persistent intrusive factor that dominates their choice of residence and lifestyle, causing them to move from their house or apartment or to avoid ordinary life events that remind them of the assault. For victims of sexual assault, prosecution may respond directly to the psychological harm of the crime. Even though timely apprehension, conviction, and incarceration of the assailant may be therapeutic for the majority of sexual assault victims, for those who live in chronic fear of retaliation or of another sexual assault, the apprehension, conviction, and incarceration of their assailant may be therapeutic, however late it occurs, if it helps reduce their fear of retaliation or repeat of the crime. For victims of sexual assault, prosecution sooner may be more therapeutic than later, but prosecution later may be more therapeutic than never.

Of course, the therapeutic consequences to victims of delayed criminal prosecution are not necessarily positive. Another body of psychological theory suggests that criminal prosecution, in particular delayed criminal prosecution, may have profound antitherapeutic effects for crime victims. Mental health professionals who do grief work to help people recover from the loss of a close friend or relative generally conclude that successful recovery requires one to confront the loss, reflect on it and on memories of the close friend or relative, and then to move on to detach from memories of the deceased.[40] Although a person may never stop grieving for the death of one who is close to that person, those who specialize in grief work maintain that it is healthy over time for the deceased to have a smaller presence in our daily life. The possibility of delayed criminal prosecution, which may send a signal encouraging crime victims to await justice, may deter this process of detachment, leaving victims stuck on the crime and their loss, much as people who have posttraumatic stress disorder (PTSD) become stuck on the trauma. Indeed, to some "the pledge never to forget until justice is done can become a pledge to refuse to recover."[41] In cases in which survivors have successfully detached from the deceased, delayed criminal prosecution may frustrate their recovery. "In a perverse sense, victims who are preoccupied with vengeance never become fully free of the pernicious influence of their victimizer."[42]

One variable that complicates assessing the effect of delayed prosecution is the social context in which these crimes are revealed.[43] Time may, of course, change this social context. The psychological effect of delayed war crimes prosecutions that reveal evidence of sexual violations of women in a culture that remains unsympathetic to women who have been sexually assaulted is not comparable to the psychological effect of delayed war crimes prosecutions that reveal evidence of torture of political activists whose cause has now triumphed. An unaltered unsympathetic social context threatens revictimization, whereas an alteration in the social structure that fostered the crime offers vindication to the victim.

How crime victims respond to the delayed prosecution of horrific crimes seems likely to be a complex interaction of a number of variables. One source of information about the long-term consequences of trauma consists of studies of Holocaust survivors. Some studies indicate that as many as half of Holocaust survivors meet the diagnostic criteria for PTSD, including sleep disorders and nightmares.[44] Even for those Holocaust survivors who do not have chronic symptoms of PTSD, loss of physical capacity due to aging, retirement, or loss of a parent or a child leaving home may serve as a stressor to trigger PTSD. Both physically and psychologically, the Holocaust experience renders elderly Holocaust survivors more vulnerable than similar-age people. Although PTSD symptoms in most groups generally tend to lessen over time, 50 years later, Holocaust survivors continue to suffer significant symptoms, including nightmares and other sleep disturbance.[45] Notwithstanding the persistence of sleep disturbances and recurrent nightmares, however, the relatively small proportion of Holocaust survivors who receive mental health care tells us something about their choice of coping strategies and willingness to be reminded of these horrors, even in a confidential setting.[46] For Holocaust survivors who have chosen to cope through denial or avoidance,[47] delayed war crimes prosecutions in which they are called to give evidence and revisit the events of the Holocaust may be an attack on their coping mechanism. Moreover, the evidence that many Holocaust survivors experience a delayed onset of PTSD or worsening of its symptoms during middle to late life as their mental and physical resilience declines[48] raises another cautionary flag about the therapeutic effect of throwing elderly victims of old crimes into the judicial system.

Any examination of the therapeutic consequences of the criminal justice system for crime victims must also account for the complaints that the criminal justice system often revictimizes crime victims by failing to acknowledge their legitimate concerns and subjecting them to rigorous questioning and lengthy delays.[49] Although there have been modest improvements, the basic structure of the modern adversarial criminal justice system in the United States, pitting the state against the defendant, and according certain basic constitutional protections to the defendant against the power of the state, ensures that the victim's therapeutic interests will invariably not be the system's paramount concern. The constitutional litmus test for criminal trials is whether they are fair to the defendant, not to the victim.[50] Thus, whatever therapeutic benefits victims enjoy from participation in the criminal justice system will be offset by their participation in a system in which they are not formally a party to and do not enjoy full decision-making authority and in which the defendant has a vested interest in attacking their credibility. Particularly in delayed prosecutions in which the prosecutorial mechanism has not achieved justice in a timely manner, as discussed above, concerns with the grief process, the combined effects of PTSD and aging, and a social context that may be unsympathetic to victims suggest that there is good reason to be concerned about the antitherapeutic consequences of prosecution.

Delayed prosecution interjects an additional layer of legal issues, such as statutes of limitation, that may derail the prosecution and its potential therapeutic benefits. Delayed prosecution increases the likelihood that victims will be shuffled from teams of prosecutors and investigators, with whom they have developed a rapport, who have retired or been transferred, to new teams of prosecutors and investigators to whom they must retell their story and establish a rapport. Moreover, delayed prosecution increases the risk of an acquittal because of the inherent problems of proof that are exacerbated in these cases, which may itself have antitherapeutic consequences. Reflective of the problems of proof inherent in delayed prosecution and its antitherapeutic potential are the prosecutions between 1959 and 1969 of 1,000 people accused of Nazi crimes, which resulted in fewer than 100 life sentences and 300 limited sentences.[51] From the perspective of a Holocaust survivor, these cases may be seen to say that even if delayed prosecution occurs, punishment is unlikely, and punishment befitting their crimes remote.

Given the absence of sound research that would make it possible to predict with any degree of precision how crime victims will react to delayed prosecution of old crimes, it is important that prosecutors address these risks and the absence of scientific answers about the psychological consequences of delayed prosecution with crime victims. In the case of delayed prosecution, crime victims whose physical or psychological pain has not driven them to take their own lives or drown themselves in a sea of alcohol or drugs have developed a coping strategy to go on with their lives. For better or worse, their existence provides evidence that they have developed a coping strategy that permits them to live another day. Delayed prosecution may support or destroy these coping strategies. We simply do not have good information at this time to predict what will occur when delayed prosecution is instituted and what may minimize or maximize the therapeutic or antitherapeutic consequences for which groups of crime victims. Because any special insights into the victim's response to delayed prosecution rest with the crime victim and because the primary effects of the delayed prosecution may be felt by the crime victim, it seems sensible to permit the crime victim to play a greater role in the decision-making process in the case of delayed prosecution than in other prosecutions.

The prosecution of Adolf Eichmann provides an example of one such accommodation. Even as the state of Israel proceeded against the architect of the Holocaust, Israeli prosecutors selected their witnesses from Holocaust survivors who volunteered to testify. No survivor who did not come forward voluntarily was asked or compelled to testify.[52] Permitting survivors to choose whether to testify gave them not only control over their role in the process, but also the opportunity to determine its likely effects on them.

It is remarkable that there appear to have been no empirical studies on the psychological effects on the victim of the process of trying and convicting the perpetrator of the offense. So in addressing the question of whether it is good for the victim to bring up offenses from the distant past, we remain firmly in the area of conjecture. With this caveat in mind, we examine two radically opposing views: one that counsels nonprosecution and an attitude of leaving well enough alone and another that sees prosecution as an integral part of healing and recovery.

One argument in favor of nonprosecution and of viewing time as a limitation on the pursuit of criminal behavior holds that the process of forgetting is essential to recovery, and that in forgetting an unpleasant experience the mind deprives that experience of its potential to cause distress. According to this view, one should let sleeping dogs lie.[53] In this view, by encouraging those who have had traumatic experiences to relive them many years later by narrating those experiences or making them the subject of a complaint, the judicial system merely condemns the victim to continued suffering. By contrast, the consensus in modern psychiatry and psychology is that stressful experiences should be talked about, that "psychologically *sleeping dogs do not lie*; past traumas do not simply pass or disappear with the passage of time."[54] In this view, the individual is liberated from the hold of the trauma by

understanding the traumatic event in the context of the individual's life and by acknowledging the meaning of this trauma. Such a quietus cannot be achieved without
a certain degree of recounting and reliving of the difficult experience. As one writer
on the treatment of trauma put it,

> Perhaps the central purpose to be achieved in the treatment of stress disorder is to
> facilitate the (eventual) fullest possible reexperiencing and recollecting of the trauma
> in the here and now . . . , the final step in the treatment process being the integration
> of all aspects of the trauma experience, both positive and negative, with the survivor's
> view of who he or she was before, during and after the trauma experience.[55]

Conclusion

If the weight of psychological opinion is in favor of confronting rather than
ignoring the stressful experiences of the past, then the question arises as to whether
the prosecution of the wrongdoer, even long delayed, could be seen as a coherent
and useful part of this program of confrontation. Certainly the prosecution of an
offense may put that offense in context. It may identify that act as a wrong and
affirm that the victim has been wronged. In that respect, it may reasonably achieve
the objective of helping the victim understand where he or she stands in relation to
the offense. The perpetrator's responsibility for the offense may be underlined, and
this may help relieve the victim of feelings of guilt that he or she somehow caused
the conduct in question. In this respect, then, prosecution can lay to rest unnecessary
and inappropriate feelings of guilt and collusion. It may also free the victim of the
wrongdoer's dominance and resulting fear. In this way, prosecution, even if delayed,
reduces an offender to size and reveals his or her true colors as an exploiter. Thus,
the victim is freed from fear. This is, of course, attractive enough in theory, but still
wanting in empirical proof.

Endnotes

1. *New directions from the field victims' rights and services for the 21st century* (Washington,
   DC: U.S. Department of Justice, Office of Justice Programs, Office for Victims of Crime,
   1998); Kent Roach, *Due process and victims' rights: The new law and politics of criminal
   justice* (Toronto, Ontario, Canada: University of Toronto Press, 1999).
2. Lawrence G. Calhoun et al., "Traumatic events and generational differences in assumptions about a just world," *Journal of Social Psychology* 138 (1998):789–791; Deborah
   A. Stowers and Mark W. Durm, "Is belief in a just world rational?" *Psychological Reports* 83 (1998):423–426.
3. *California v. Franklin,* rev'd *Franklin v. Duncan,* 884 F.Supp. 1435 (N.D. Cal. 1995).
4. Gerard E. Lynch, "The lawyer as informer," *Duke Law Journal* 1986 (1986):491–547,
   at 524 ("We generally regard it as an appropriate exercise of prosecutorial discretion
   when a prosecutor takes the victim's attitude into account. The victim's attitude toward
   the crime is seen as an appropriate factor in assessing its seriousness and, indeed, may
   be the critical factor in the decision whether or not to prosecute if the crime is otherwise
   at the margin of social attention").
5. See David B. Wexler and Bruce J. Winick, Eds. *Law in a therapeutic key: Developments
   in therapeutic jurisprudence* (Durham, NC: Carolina Academic Press, 1996).

6. Richard P. Weibe, "The mental health implications of crime victim's rights." In *Law in a therapeutic key: Developments in therapeutic jurisprudence,* David B. Wexler and Bruce J. Winick, Eds. (Durham, NC: Carolina Academic Press, 1996).

7. *Id.*

8. Paul Zielbauer, "Cold War villains unpunished/low conviction rate in German courts," *Newsday,* May 29, 1997, at A17.

9. Robert H. Reid, "Libya presses its case for end to sanctions over Pan Am bombing," *AP Worldstream,* Mar. 20, 1998.

10. Brandon Hamber, "Living with the legacy of impunity: Lessons for South Africa about truth, justice and crime in Brazil." *Unisa Latin American Report* 13(2) (1997):4–16.

11. The Department of Justice Bureau of Justice Statistics 1995 Crimes Victimization Survey found that 63% of all crimes are not reported to the police, whereas 31% of rape–sexual assaults are reported to the police.

12. Weibe, *Law in a therapeutic key,* at 224.

13. Patricia A. Cluss et al. "The rape victim: Psychological correlates of participation in the legal process," *Criminal Justice & Behavior* 10 (1983):342–357.

14. Arthur J. Lurigio and Patricia A. Resick, "Healing the psychological wounds of criminal victimization: Predicting postcrime distress and recovery." In *Victims of crime: Problems, policies and programs,* Arthur J. Lurigio, Wesley Skogan, and Robert Davis, Eds. (Thousand Oaks, CA: Sage).

15. "Executive summary 1985. Final report of the APA Task Force on the Victims of Crime and Violence," *American Psychologist* 40 (1985):107–112, at 108.

16. See chapter 2.

17. Meredith B. McGuire, "Words of power: Personal empowerment and healing," *Culture, Medicine & Psychiatry* 7 (1983):221–240, at 222; Peter L. Berger and Richard J. Neuhaus, *To empower people: The role of mediating structures in public policy* (Washington, DC: American Enterprise Institute for Public Policy Research, 1977) at 7 (discussing the ways in which institutions controlled by faceless people have resulted in a feeling of powerlessness in modern society); Anita Hodgkiss, "Note. Petitioning and the empowerment theory of practice," *Yale Law Journal* 96 (1987):569–592 (arguing that the radical lawyer's focus should be to encourage individual and collective empowerment).

18. Meredith B. McGuire, "Words of power: Personal empowerment and healing," *Culture, Medicine & Psychiatry* 7 (1983):221–240, at 222; Peter E. S. Freund, *The civilized body: Social domination, control, and health* (Philadelphia: Temple University Press, 1982).

19. This use of the judicial system to reshape personal relationships was observed by Laura Nader in her study of the Mexican Zapotec courts. Laura Nader, *Styles of court procedure: To make the balance, in law and culture in society* (Berkeley: University of California Press, 1969) at 69. "The Zapotec ideal is not an 'eye for an eye' but rather what restores personal relations to equilibrium," *Id.* at 73.

20. Deborah Hensler et al. *Compensation for accidental injuries in the United States* (Santa Monica, CA: RAND Institute for Civil Justice, 1991) at 147.

21. Glanville Williams and B. A. Hepple, *Foundations of the law of torts* (London: Butterworths, 1976) at 116.

22. Lynda M. Sagrestano, "The use of power and influence in a gendered world," *Psychology of Women Quarterly* 16 (1992):439–447, at 439.

23. See Holly J. Manley, "Comment, civil compensation for the victim of rape," *Cooley Law Review* 7 (1990):193–211, at 202.

24. Nora West, "Note. Rape in the criminal law and the victim's tort alternative: A feminist analysis," *University of Toronto Faculty Law Review* 50 (1992):96–118, at 114; Bruce Feldthusen, "The civil action for sexual battery: Therapeutic jurisprudence," *Ottawa Law Review* 25 (1993):203–234. *See,* generally, Dale T. Miller and Carol A. Porter, "Self-blame in victims of violence," *Journal of Social Issues* 39 (1983):139–152 (delineating types of victim self-blame and discussing their implication on the victimization process).

25. Ariane Brunet and Stephanie Rousseau, "Acknowledging violations, struggling against impunity: Women's rights as human rights." In *Campaign against impunity: Portrait and plan of action* (Montreal, Quebec, Canada: Centre for Human Rights and Democratic Development, 1997).

26. Joan H. Liem et al., "The need for power in women who were sexually abused as children," *Psychology of Women Quarterly* 16 (1992):467–480, at 468.

27. *Id.* Similarly, "the rules that battered women try desperately to follow become established in a pattern of domination and control by the enforcement mechanism used by the batterer." Karla Fischer et al., "The culture of battering and the role of mediation in domestic violence cases," *Southern Methodist University Law Review* 46 (1993):2117–2174, at 2131.

28. David Finkelhor and Angela Browne, "The traumatic impact of child sexual abuse: A conceptualization," *American Journal of Orthopsychiatry* 55 (1985):530–541, at 532.

29. Gail S. Goodman et al. "Testifying in court," *Monographs of the Society for Research in Child Development* 57(5) (1992): 6.

30. *Id.*

31. Stevan M. Weine et al., "Testimony psychotherapy in Bosnian refugees: A pilot study," *American Journal of Psychiatry* 155 (1998):1720–1726.

32. *Id.* at 1723.

33. *Id.* at 1720.

34. See Federal Rules of Evidence 611(a): "The court shall exercise reasonable control over the mode and order of interrogating witnesses and presenting evidence so as to . . . (3) protect witnesses from harassment or undue embarrassment" and comparable state rules.

35. Daniel W. Shuman, "The psychology of compensation in tort law," *Kansas Law Review* 43 (1994):39–77.

36. For example, whereas the parents of South African anti-apartheid activist Steven Biko, killed by government security forces, opposed the Truth and Reconciliation Commission (TRC) and amnesty for their son's killers, the parents of Amy Biehl, a 26-year-old American Fulbright scholar killed by Blacks in the waning days of apartheid, supported the TRC and forgave their daughter's killers. See Donald S. Shriver, *The Christian Century* 115(23), Aug. 1998, at 772.

37. Paula McMahon, "Jury finds Penalver guilty in five year old triple slaying: 'Yes, yes, yes' verdicts relieve victims' families," *Sun Sentinel*, Nov. 13, 1999, at 1A.

38. Marilyn Augus, "Former Vichy official flees France," *Austin American Statesman*, Oct. 21, 1999, at A24.

39. Patricia A. Frazier and Eugene Borgida, "Rape trauma syndrome: A review of case law and psychological research," *Law & Human Behavior* 16 (1992):293–311.

40. Margaret Stroebe and Wolfgang Stroebe, "Does 'grief work' work?" *Journal of Consulting and Clinical Psychology* 59 (1991):479–482.

41. Nancy Weinberg, "Self-blame, other blame, and desire for revenge: Factors in recovery and bereavement," *Death Studies* 18 (1994):585–593.

42. Seymour L. Halleck, "Vengeance and victimization," *Victimology* 5 (1980):99–109, at 107.

43. Lynne N. Henderson, "The wrongs of victim's rights," *Stanford Law Review* 37 (1985): 937–1021.

44. Inge Hyman, "Post-traumatic stress disorder in the elderly." In *Psychological trauma: A development approach*, Dora Black et al., Eds. (London: Gaskell, 1997).

45. Jules Rosen et al., "Sleep disturbances in survivors of the Nazi Holocaust," *American Journal of Psychiatry* 148 (1991):62–66.

46. Klaus Kuch and Brian J. Cox, "Symptoms of PTSD in 124 survivors of the Holocaust," *American Journal of Psychiatry* 149 (1992):337–340.

47. Michael J. Salamon, "Denial and acceptance: Coping mechanisms," *Clinical Gerontologist* 14 (1994):17–25.

48. Petra G. H. Aarts and Wybrand Op Den Velde, "Prior traumatization and the process of aging: Theory and clinical implications." In *Traumatic stress: The effects of overwhelming experience on mind, body, and society*, Bessel A. Van der Kolk et al., Eds. (New York: Guilford Press, 1996).

49. Arthur J. Lurigio and Patricia A. Resick, "Healing the psychological wounds of criminal victimization: Predicting postcrime distress and recovery." In *Victims of crime: Problems, policies and programs,* Arthur J. Lurigio, Wesley Skogan, and Robert Davis, Eds. (Thousand Oaks, CA: Sage, 1990) at 60.

50. See, e.g., *Booth v. Maryland,* 482 U.S. 496 (1987): A finding that the introduction of a victim impact statement in capital sentencing determination violated defendant's rights under the 8th Amendment of the Constitution.

51. Carlos Santiago Nino, *Radical evil on trial* (New Haven, CT: Yale University Press, 1996) at 9.

52. Hannah Arendt, *Eichmann in Jerusalem: A report on the banality of evil* (New York: Viking Press, 1993) at 203.

53. For a discussion of these issues in the context of the Truth and Reconciliation Commission in South Africa, *see* Brandon Hamber, "Do sleeping dogs lie? The psychological implications of the Truth and Reconciliation Commission in South Africa," seminar paper at the Centre for the Study of Violence and Reconciliation, July 26, 1995.

54. *Id.* at 3.

55. R. M. Scurfield, "Post-trauma stress assessment and treatment: Overview and formulations." In *Trauma and its wake: The study and treatment of post-traumatic stress disorder* (New York: Brunner/Mazel, 1985, Vol. 1), at 245, 246.

Chapter 8
JUSTICE AND FORGIVENESS:
A Delicate Balance

The past is a different country.[1]

Our concern in this book has been with the past and with the hold that its wrongs may have over us. This hold may be powerful, as is shown by the tenacity with which many are prepared to pursue justice or by the effort that they expend on the narrative reconstruction of past events. But the past potentially brings with it a measure of pain: The reliving or contemplation of past wrongs may rekindle painful memories of suffering and loss, and it may prolong such memories beyond their natural span. An appropriate panacea for this pain might be to sever it from its source —by demoting the importance of the past. This, it seems, is far from simple: People are intimately connected with their past, both as individuals and as members of a community, and, what is more, they need the past to create their sense of personal and collective self. Without a historical sense, they cannot understand their current selves, and indeed many of their actions are only fully intelligible in the context of their past.

The Role of the Past in Defining the Present

Both morality and the law tend to take a "snapshot" view of human action. People look at acts in isolation and assess them on the basis of their effect and the intentions behind them. Punishment, as a consequence, tends to be determined on the moral features of the particular act in question rather than on the meaning of the act in the context of the actor's life. The acts of women who kill their partners or spouses at a moment when they are not immediately threatening to do the women harm can be understood as straightforward instances of homicide and are dealt with accordingly. In many cases, however, these acts are the result of a long and complex history of violent abuse, and to see these acts outside of this history may be to misunderstand their nature.[2] In such cases, the woman's past may make some sense of the act, even if it does not excuse it. This need has increasingly been recognized by those courts that have permitted defenses based on self-defense or provocation in such cases.[3] Traditionally, pleas of provocation were available in criminal law only if the defendant's response followed immediately on a seriously provocative act.[4] This would exclude the defense in the case of abused women who could not point to an act of provocation immediately preceding their attack on their tormentor. This limitation on placing the battered woman's act in context has been addressed by courts that have either recognized the responsibility-limiting effect of battered woman syndrome or that have been prepared to extend the notion of provocation to include the whole history of the relationship between the parties. Cumulative provocation, built up over many months or years of abuse, may then be taken into account in mitigating the seriousness of the crime. This demonstrates a more historically sensitive interpretation of the criminal act and represents a move away from the "snapshot," single-instant approach.[5] Similarly, application of the standard by which the reasonableness of battered women who kill their partners are to be judged has increasingly included the experiences common to battered women.[6]

Awareness of the past affords people a more sophisticated view of human action; in many situations, it is only by taking into account the historical background that people can reach an adequate understanding of actor and action. Yet the past does not provide the entire explanation of action: People cannot lose sight of themselves as autonomous actors, acting within the framework of the choices that they make. If the past is to be given too great a role in the explanation of action, then they run the risk of falling into the familiar determinist trap in which events and experiences take center stage, pushing the human actor into the wings. There is a tension between the view of human actors as individually responsible agents, solely accountable for their acts, and the view of people as historically determined actors. Proponents of this latter view would caution us to take into account that people act in a historical context, according to the mores of their time and in the context of contemporary events. It is anachronistic, according to this view, to apply the standards and understanding of our own time to past acts. This has important implications for the prosecution of old crimes.

There are two dangers. One is to give too little weight to historical distance and to judge the past by the standards of the present. Those who do so may reflexively condemn past acts that conflict with contemporary moral standards. Judging the criminal responsibility of the East German border guards charged with shooting those fleeing to the West, without taking into account the existence of the Cold War and the military regime in which these soldiers served, would risk ignoring the full historical context of their actions.[7]

The other danger is to give excessive prominence to the historical context, failing to leave any room for individual responsibility. Officials of Vichy, France during World War II benefited from this approach. There was a widely held view in France that many such people were merely victims of historical circumstance and could not be condemned for their collaborationist activities. It is only comparatively recently that opinion in France has addressed the uncomfortable truths about responsibility for actions taken during this period.[8] The danger is that by attempting to understand the background, people lose sight of the fact that certain moral standards are properly historically transferable.

If people are to make moral judgments about the past, it is important to avoid these extremes. The particular worldview of the time must be taken into account to understand people's motives, but having taken this step we can still assess individuals on the basis of their dispositions and intentions. The surrounding circumstances, then, may perform no more and no less than the role that they perform in our assessment of our contemporaries. Although many regimes have justified their resorting to torture to protect society from some greater evil, it is important that these purported historical justifications do not obscure individual responsibility for these acts. Our conversations about the past may impinge on our conversations about the present. If people condone past torture on the ground that people thought it permissible at the time, they compromise their ability to condemn it today. It is for this reason that their sense of the moral present is intimately caught up in their view of the past.

At the broader social level, people use their understanding of the past to chart their future. They have a notion of what their political community was in the past, how it reached its present position, and how it related in the past to others. This historical perspective is an important element in a state's sense of identity. A state that lacked a sense of the past would be little more than a random collection of individuals, bereft of a common culture. We would not expect the individuals who composed it to share a sense of community.

But if a sense of the past can enrich, it can also be burdensome. If people allow the past to dominate, they may find that it has an immutable agenda of its own. A nation dominated by the past would be condemned to refight old battles and never progress beyond them. An individual dominated by the past would be condemned to dwell on old issues and arguments and make little moral or psychological progress. To integrate the past appropriately, it must serve to highlight our choices, not to restrict them.

Imagine a society in which it did not matter what people had done, in which all that mattered was the present. Such a society would be unworkable, at the least because it could not sustain a notion of accountability or responsibility. In such a society there would be no blame, no calling to account, and no punishment. People could do whatever they liked, confident that they would face no repercussions for their actions. No society, of course, operates in this way. Every society has its notions of responsibility, requiring that people be called to account for past actions. Every society judges people on the basis of what they have done, not simply for who they are. People follow this pattern, intuitively, in their social dealings as well.

People also understand intuitively that the past can be a hindrance in their current lives. They have legitimate uses for the past, but they need to maintain a sense of separation from what has gone before. Not only do they have to recognize the fact of change—in people and in institutions—but they must also be ready to put the past behind us. Through the use of statutes of limitations, following the passage of time, people no longer consider certain events relevant.[9] These become events that no longer matter to them legally, events that are, in an important sense, dead.

That is how it should be. There are pathological attitudes toward the past that may have the effect of either minimizing its role or giving it prominence. Both attitudes have their perils. If we minimize the importance of the past and live with an extremely short memory, we risk misjudgments. We may, for example, place our trust in people whose record, if we chose to unearth it, would speak eloquently to their untrustworthiness. A politician hounded out of office for corruption could subsequently successfully seek re-election several years later simply because his past is dismissed.[10] It would be the height of folly for a nation with a history of political extremism—whether of the left or the right—to fail to remind itself of its past.

A striking insight into this risk is in the late 20th-century German media's graphical reminders to the public of the horrors of the Nazi regime.[11] Liberal opinion in Germany has consistently sought to remind the public of what happened during the National Socialist period. At a popular level this reminder took the form of vivid accounts in newspapers and journals of suffering at the hands of the Nazis. At a more rarified level there was an intense debate among historians as to the "normalization" of Nazism within the context of 20th-century German history. Proponents of normalization argued that Nazism could be understood as a response to particular historical pressures. Opponents of normalization were adamant that the abnormality and essential criminality of Nazism be kept in clear focus, fearing that many crimes could be redefined as matters of normal mass psychology. The desire to preserve the discrete memory of Nazism should not be seen as an unduly guilt-ridden response; it demonstrates, rather, a determination that the public should not forget the calamity of fascism. The remembrance of the past in contemporary Germany is vital to the political health of a country that recognizes the existence of dangerous currents within its polity. As a result, the country arguably enjoys a better moral position than that occupied by those states that have not confronted their past.

Another form of pathological relationship to the past, characterized by undue attachment to it, similarly risks distorting current relationships. Again at the national level, there are many examples from which one could choose. Historical wrongs, paraded and carefully cultivated, can be a powerful source of hatred and a fuel for conflict. The prolonged suffering of Northern Ireland demonstrates this. It is a re-markable feature of political debate in Northern Ireland that both sides to the conflict make such extensive use of past injustice and past wrongs, notwithstanding efforts to focus the political debates on current concerns.[12] A political discussion over the rights and wrongs of the partition of Ireland may rapidly descend to an exchange of wrongs committed many years—sometimes centuries—previously. The Balkans pro-vide another compelling example of the power of historical animosity to shape the present. It came as a surprise to many to discover at the end of the 20th century that the events of the 14th century played an active role in current ethnic disputes in the Balkans.[13] It would be impossible to understand many of the animosities in the Balkans if one were unaware of the historical experience of the various peoples and of the extent to which they define themselves as distinct groups on the basis of this experience.

What we see here is precisely the tension that permeates the debate over the prosecution of old crimes. Criminal justice is about calling people to account for their acts. Necessarily, therefore, it looks to the past. As seen throughout our earlier discussion, however, there is a sense in which the passage of time ameliorates the effects of many human wrongs. At some point, their effect may no longer be felt, the pain they cause may no longer be experienced; in short, with the passage of time they may lose their claim to our attention. Recognizing this, society must seek an approach to put past wrongs behind it in a way that will not offend its sense of justice or undermine the authority of the moral and legal rules by which people live. This task requires that people distinguish the recent, morally relevant past from its more distant, morally irrelevant counterpart. How is this to be done?

Distinguishing the Morally Relevant Past

The granting of amnesty is one way of drawing the line. Some amnesties may be motivated by simple convenience; for example, taxing authorities may find that granting an amnesty on prosecution is useful in encouraging the payment of past-due taxes.[14] Other amnesties are inspired by a spirit of forgiveness. Where the crimes that have been committed are on a large scale in the context of political or social disputes, amnesty provides a useful way of distancing from the past. The justification for amnesty in this setting may be the interest that society has in encouraging a new set of relations in which resentment and a sense of grievance will be downplayed.

This device has been used as a means of promoting social healing and political reconciliation in the transformations of regimes in many countries, as noted in chapter 5. The crimes subject to amnesty may have individual victims, but what distinguishes them is their political and social motivation. It signals a shift in society's focus from the past to the future and implicitly states that the crime is a product of circumstances that have now changed.

Another approach to distinguishing the morally relevant and irrelevant past is to draw arbitrary lines, imposing predetermined statutes of limitation for classes of offenses. The imposition of a time limit within which prosecution must be initiated or abandoned altogether at least makes the position clear. The state knows that it must prepare and present its case in a timely fashion that is clearly prescribed by a predetermined rule. The victim is required to make known his grievance against the perpetrator within a fixed time. Furthermore, the defendant is relieved of the anxiety and uncertainty of an indeterminate prospect of prosecution. Drawing a line distinguishes, albeit somewhat crudely, between the relevant and irrelevant past. Although rules that draw lines imposing predetermined statutes of limitation for classes of offenses may encourage parties to argue over the precise application of a rule and its exceptions, they do not encourage the parties or the court to address the continued moral relevance of the wrongdoing. The expiration of the statute of limitations or the application of an exception to it tells us nothing about the circumstances of a particular victim and the harm that the victim may continue to suffer. For example, tolling the statute of limitations in a child sexual abuse prosecution because the perpetrator has left the jurisdiction says nothing about the need for retribution in this case or the therapeutic consequences of prosecution to the victim.

The passage of time, of course, casts doubt on our ability to reach accurate determinations of criminal responsibility. Thus, statutes of limitation, at least in theory, serve to limit prosecutions that would present greater evidential problems. Again, however, the wooden application of statutes of limitations fails to make case-specific assessments of problems of proof. They do not, for example, bar timely prosecution of child sex abuse cases tainted by suggestive questioning, whereas they do bar long-delayed prosecution in child sexual abuse cases in which there is no reason to suspect that suggestive questioning has occurred. Limitations encourage timely prosecution, resulting in witnesses being asked to relate more recent memories, but they arbitrarily bar prosecution of events that took place many years ago, even if there is good reason to believe that the evidence against the accused is accurate.

Another approach to distinguishing between the morally relevant and irrelevant past, which is widely accepted by common-law jurisdictions other than the United States, is to have no statute of limitations but to make case-specific decisions about whether the passage of time would result in fundamental unfairness. The Canadian cases discussed in chapter 4 are examples of this approach. Although producing results tailored to the facts and circumstances of the individual case, this rule obviously lacks the certainty and predictability that statutes of limitation bring. It is not difficult to see the problems of proof presented by the prosecution of sexual assaults alleged to have been committed more than 40 years ago. The approach of a fixed statute of limitation arbitrarily tells victims that insofar as the criminal justice stem is concerned, they must consign these events to the past. The absence of a limitation period leaves open the possibility that victims may pursue these issues through the criminal justice system years or even decades later. Whether this ap-

proach offers victims a necessary therapeutic alternative or encourages them to remain pathologically focused on events that occurred many years ago is far from
clear. For now, all that we can conclude is that for some crime victims, prosecution,
even delayed by many years, is therapeutic, whereas for others, delayed prosecution
holds no benefit or may even be counterproductive. If there is no predictable therapeutic benefit in either of the alternatives of limitation or nonlimitation, then justifications for either approach must be found elsewhere. To do this, we look to the
issue of punishment.

How does deterrence, which is an important justification for criminal punishment, relate to the approach taken to limitations? An indefinite prospect of prosecution, on the surface, seems more likely to deter. The possibility of prosecution
unlimited by time seems to convey a message to criminals that maximizes their
incentive to comply with legal rules. Thus, the decision to exclude homicide from
the bar of the statute of limitations says to would-be murderers that they can never
escape prosecution. There is no research that links an indefinite prospect of prosecution with increased deterrence, however. It may be that in the face of fixed statutes
of limitation, law enforcement is more zealous in prosecuting criminal conduct in a
timely fashion than where fixed limitation periods are absent, resulting in greater
deterrence. We do not know and thus cannot confidently conclude that approach to
limitations will further the goal of deterrence.

Retribution is more complex. Fixed periods of limitation leave open the prospect
that individual offenders will escape the punishment they may be thought to deserve.
If we impose a statute of limitation on war crimes, a war criminal may, on that
account, escape the punishment that is deserved. Although the passage of time has
a moderating effect on the call for retribution, statutes of limitation are an imprecise
tool to measure the need for retribution. Limitation periods only address classes of
cases and do not necessarily account for the degree of wrongdoing or the harm that
occurred in a particular case. It is not uncommon in a sexual abuse case to find that
the perpetrator has repeatedly abused the victim over a considerable period of time,
as illustrated by the Kos case discussed in chapter 1. The heinousness of this pattern
of conduct and its need for retribution is not acknowledged in the running of the
statute of limitations. The limitation period would typically run from the date of the
last offense or the victim's attaining of the age of majority and would take no account
of the scale of offending. When this broad-brush approach leads to the perception
that the criminal justice system is prepared to ignore the magnitude of the wrong, it
weakens the moral authority of the criminal law. This is a devastating message.

The law must make a statement about wrongs that are matters of current concern,
whereas at the same time it must consign to the "inactive" past those wrongs that
are no longer of current moral importance. It must punish old crimes in cases in
which this is justified, and it must facilitate and encourage forgiveness in cases in
which this is appropriate. These tasks may at times appear incompatible. Yet a reasonable working compromise may be achieved. The most desirable policy is to adopt
a system of limitations that is, first, generous to the victim in the length of periods
applied, provided, of course, that reliable evidence is available to permit the case to
be tried fairly. The second requirement is that such a system should be sensitive to
the individual claims of the various forms of crime and, in particular, would allow
for exceptions based on the magnitude of the crime.

Part of the compromise must be the exclusion from limitation provisions of certain crimes that by reason of their seriousness, must remain indefinitely open to prosecution. The most common example is homicide, which, under existing provisions, is usually excluded from the statute of limitations. War crimes are another example, although they frequently involve homicide and would, for this reason, remain open to prosecution at any point. These exceptions are so broadly endorsed that it would seem that they express an almost universal conviction. But why should these crimes be treated exceptionally? One response is that the sense of outrage in these cases survives the passage of time. Taking a human life is not an act that one can readily consign to the "irrelevant" past. Homicide survives the passage of time as a matter of moral concern because society attributes a high value to human life. The prohibition against killing requires a particular emphasis, and it is usually given this emphasis in criminal justice by the invocation of the supreme penalty, capital punishment, or life imprisonment. In the case of war crimes or crimes of genocide, the significance of what happened is so profound that the pain persists, sometimes over generations. It is in recognition of this prolonged pain that the law regards the wrong as a continuing one until it is expiated by a proper judicial response. In the area of genocidal crimes, we touch on an issue that is inevitably of immense sensitivity, and we must be conscious of the fact that the monstrosity of such crimes demands a response. We simply cannot remove them to the irrelevant past because that would be seen as a denial of the suffering of the victims and a turning away from what is a central moral lesson of this time.

Remembrance and Forgiveness

Of course before an act can be forgotten it must be remembered. The process of remembering historical events may have a political component. Thus, it is pertinent to inquire whose memory people are discussing. Not all genocide campaigns have lodged in the memory of those unaffected by these acts. The slaughters perpetrated by the Zulu's under Chaka in the 19th century are not widely remembered as genocides around the globe, nor is the genocide of the Armenians by the Turks, the depredations of Stalin, or the extermination of the Tasmanian aborigines by British settlers in the 19th century. Increased historical understanding and cultural sensitivity is now resulting in broader remembrance of some of these crimes.[15] Their memories are politically and psychologically constructed.

Keeping alive the memory of past wrongs should not obscure the role of forgiveness. We argued that there are powerful reasons for the exercise of forgiveness. In an important sense, a system of limitations endorses this view. Imposing an end to recrimination opens the way to reassessment of how we stand in relation to a past wrong. The logic of this reassessment will often point in the direction of transcending current feelings of resentment.

To forgive a wrong, however, is not necessarily to forget that wrong. It is possible to forgive a wrong and yet retain a clear memory of it. Similarly, forgiveness does not imply that one has condoned the act; no rule, moral or legal, is compromised by its exercise. A model that has elevated the role of forgiveness is the South African Truth and Reconciliation Commission, which has attempted a constructive compromise between those caught up in past wrongs, both as perpetrators and victims. Although rejecting retribution for politically motivated crimes committed in support of and in opposition to apartheid, the South African system does not involve unconditional amnesty. Instead, it insists on a full recounting of wrongs as a precondition of amnesty.[16] In this way, there is an acknowledgment of the victim's suffering, which is painstakingly recited into the record. On these grounds, the suggestion that the wrongs of the past are being treated lightly is officially refuted, although, as pointed out, not all victims have found the process an adequate response to their suffering. Compromises of this sort are inevitably painful, but many have accepted less than a full measure of justice as the price of reconciliation and national healing.

Even if this solution eventually works in South Africa, it cannot necessarily be applied in other contexts. The South African experiment is the result of a unique combination of factors. Set against the background of a characteristic African attitude to dispute resolution that downplays retribution and emphasizes community consensus, the Truth and Reconciliation Commission was part of a broad, pragmatic compromise that recognized the country's need to end the bloodshed and transform itself to an economically viable democracy.[17] But the Truth and Reconciliation Commission approach raises the possibility of creative attempts to deal with the crimes of the past. People's basic sense of justice requires that they hold individuals accountable for what they have done, yet an unwillingness to forgive can trap a person in cycles of accusation and recrimination from which he or she can find it difficult to extricate him- or herself. The task of a fair and therapeutic criminal justice system is to seek out that elusive balance that recognizes this danger but that at the same time is not deaf to the reasonable needs of victims.

A Delicate Balance

The difficulty is deciding which victim needs are reasonable. There has been considerable interest in the claims of victims, to which the law has often turned a deaf ear. Practical measures to correct this have included victim support services and a greater role for victims in criminal prosecutions. In other areas the law has been more aware of the status of people as victims of abuse, harassment, and discrimination. Real hidden suffering has been given a greater voice. Yet there are limits to the room one can give to blame. One objection to the expansion of the ranks of victim is that it may lead to a devaluation of the concept of being a victim and a failure to take victims' claims seriously. Another concern is that this expansion weakens notions of personal responsibility. Blaming others for all our misfortunes discourages a proper sense of personal responsibility. A culture that encourages blame also runs the risk of being unduly focused on the past.

But we do need blame. We need it to identify wrongdoing, and we need it to focus our attention on questions of right and wrong. Although we can understand forgiveness as a virtue, this understanding must be qualified by a recognition of the legitimate role of moral anger. Blame should be properly located in society to allow it to discharge these vital moral functions while avoiding a recrimination-dominated society. The way in which the law fixes the occasions of blame may play a major role in shaping our general social conception of those important human institutions. The law is a gatekeeper; it admits some grounds for blame and rejects others. Its task in determining the effect that the passage of time has on blameworthiness is, as seen, one that requires a careful balancing process.

One of the difficulties inherent in this balancing is the fact that there are two distinct interests to be taken into account: the interest of the law in doing justice to the individual defendant and the individual complainant (the individual interest) and the broader interest that the community may have in the use of the law as a means of recording and vindicating certain more general values (the social interest). The individual interest is the day-to-day concern of the criminal justice system. From this perspective, the important concern is to provide a legal response to a wrong committed by one person on another. In responding to this, the law seeks to achieve a just result by ensuring that there is an equitable balance between the prosecution and the defense and by ensuring that the criminal courts do not behave oppressively. In the light of these concerns, we can see why there should be a point at which the crimes of the past become no longer cognizable by the courts. This is a legal decision, heavily influenced by considerations of procedural fairness. In the purely individual context, too, society may opt for forgiveness after a period, which again may be a decision based on what is thought to be the best course for those most immediately involved in the crime.

The social interest involves different considerations, and may point to a very different result. Criminal trials have broad social significance and make statements that go beyond the condemnation of individual wrongs. This is the vision of the criminal law as theater or at least as a forum for the assertion of certain values. A high-profile trial, with its attendant publicity, may be a vehicle for communicating a political or social message. It may also provide a formal means of recording history.

It is possible to view many instances of the trial of old crimes as examples of social interest trials, prompted, to an extent, by politics. Certainly some sexual abuse cases can be understood in this way. We have witnessed a profound change in the way in which society responded to sexual crimes in the last quarter of the 20th century. The legal understanding of these acts as instances of aggravated assaults was replaced by an awareness of these offenses as examples of sexual exploitation, to be viewed within a context of unequal relationships between men and women, between adults and children, and between the empowered and disempowered. This led to the removal of many procedural hurdles, to the successful prosecution of such offenses, and to a willingness to accept that there was a far higher incidence of sexual abuse than had previously been thought to exist. Sexual abuse and assault trials are therefore often seen as mere exemplars of the wider problem. There is intense interest in the outcome and in the sentencing, as if the court were not merely pronouncing on the guilt of the defendant on trial but on the guilt of sexual abusers in general. This has imparted a political connotation to these trials. There are, then, many people who see the criminal justice system as a means of publicly vindicating personal and social wrong. The trial then becomes a way of saying "this not only happened to me, but it also happens to others." Those who are victims may wish to record their suffering in this way, and they may be encouraged to do so by support groups and campaigners who praise the courage of those who come forward to complain of wrongs against them, often many years after the wrong.

War crimes provide another example of criminal justice as political theater. We stressed the important deterrent argument in favor of war crime trials, but it is impossible to escape the political element that characterizes many of these events. At their worst, these are victors' justice and are highly selective in their focus. At their best, they provide an important means by which sense can be made of confusing loss, and a consoling history can be forged for victims to contextualize their suffering. Here again, however, there may be a conflict between the individual and social concerns of criminal justice. Where the crime charged is committed under orders—as in the case of the East German border guards—a sense of individual justice balks at the punishing of young men under military discipline, even if the defense of coercion has consistently been refused in such trials in the past.

Our response to the problem of the pursuit of old crimes must take into account both the individual and the social dimensions. The adoption of a purely individual perspective may obscure the social and political context in which these crimes are viewed. To allow, then, evidentiary concerns or considerations of oppression to decide the matter may be to take too limited a view. But equally, to pursue the social objective is to ignore the important considerations of justice that must be preserved. A fair trial, after all, is a matter of human rights, and society cannot afford to allow the criminal justice system to be used in the pursuit of partisan political goals. We should bear in mind, too, that a proper sense of justice may involve not only a willingness to delve into the past, but also a sense of when it is right to put the past to rest and to counsel forgiveness. At a certain point, recrimination becomes as disfiguring as wrongdoing itself.

Endnotes

1. Leslie Poles Hartley, *The go-between* (London: Hamish Hamilton, 1953) at 3.
2. Joyce Klemperer, "Symposium on reconceptualizing violence against women by intimate partners: Critical issues: Programs for battered woman—What works," *Albany Law Review* 58 (1995):1171–1190.
3. For a critical discussion of the law's response to provocation, see Victoria Nourse, "Passion's progress: Modern law reform and the provocation defense," *Yale Law Journal* 106 (1997):1331–1448.
4. Jeremy Horder, *Provocation and responsibility* (Oxford, England: Clarendon Press, 1992).
5. Andrew Taslitz, "Myself alone: Individualizing justice through psychological character evidence," *Maryland Law Review* 59 (1993):1–120.
6. For a striking Canadian example, see *R. v. Lavallee*, S.C.R. 852 (1990).
7. The background to these cases is discussed in Tina Rosenberg, *The haunted land: Facing Europe's ghosts after communism* (New York: Vintage, 1995) at 261–305.
8. Alain Ruscio, Ed., *Oublier nos crimes. L'amnesie nationale, une specificite Francais?* [Forgetting our crimes. National amnesia, a French specialty?] (Paris, France: Editions Autrement, 1994).
9. See chapter 4.
10. See, e.g., Debra Dickerson, "Leaving D.C.: Do we deserve Marian Barry?" *The New Republic,* June 17, 1996, at 18.
11. John Paul Teschke, *Nazis, decent people, and propagandists: Controversies regarding the restoration of Nazi influences in postwar West Germany* (Ann Arbor, MI: UMI Dissertation Services, 1995); Jeffrey Herf, *Divided memory: The Nazi past in the two Germanys* (Cambridge, MA: Harvard University Press, 1997).
12. Allen Feldman, *Formations of violence: The narrative of the body and political terror in Northern Ireland* (Chicago: University of Chicago Press, 1991).
13. Thomas Thomas, *Serbia under Milosovic* (London: Hurst, 1999).
14. "Italian Budget Committee approves tax amnesty," *Reuters Financial Service,* Apr. 29, 1997, Tuesday, Bc cycle.

15. Jeremy Waldron, "Superseding historic injustice," *Ethics* 103 (1992):4–28.

16. David Yutar and Beauregard Tromp, "South Africa; The Biko, Benzien amnesty poser," *Africa News Service,* Feb. 22, 1999.

17. Archbishop Tutu's observation is telling: "If the security forces thought that they were going to be up for the high jump we would not have had a negotiated settlement, that is the price that had to be paid, and yes, the victims and survivors are probably asked a second time and to be willing—if this high price had not been paid this country would have gone up in flames." Archbishop Desmond Tutu, interview with Michael Ignatieff, "Getting away with murder," Special Correspondent Programs, BBC2.

TABLE OF AUTHORITIES

International Laws, Regulations, and Rules

International

G.A. Res. 2391, U.N. GAOR, 23d Sess., Supp. No. 18, at 40, U.N. Doc. A/RES/
2391 (1968), 754 U.N.T.S. No. 73, 8 I.L.M. 68, ch. 4, fn. 23

T.S. No. 82, 13 I.L.M. 540, ch. 4, fn. 24

Belgium

Belgian Senate Resolution 1997–1998, Resolution 1–736/3, ch. 1, fn. 20

South Africa

Constitution of the Republic of South Africa, 1993, Act No. 200 of 1993, ch. 1,
fn. 16

Promotion of National Unity and Reconciliation Act, No. 34 of 1995, ch. 1, fn. 17

United States Laws, Regulations, and Rules

Federal

U.S. Constitutional Amendment 21 § 2, ch. 5, fn. 37

Executive Order No. 11,967, 3 C.F.R. § 1 (1978), ch. 5, fn. 16

28 C.F.R. § 1.2 (1998), ch. 5, fn. 30

State

Ala. Code § 13A-13–2 (1998), ch. 5, fn. 7

Ariz. Rev. Stat. § 13–1408 (1998), ch. 5, fn. 7

Colo. Rev. Stat. § 18–6-501 (1997), ch. 5, fn. 7

Tex. Code Crim. P. art. 12.01 (1999), ch. 4, fns. 9, 10

International Cases

Australia

D. P. P. v. Polyukhovich, Supreme Court of South Australia, Dec. 22, 1992, ch. 4, fn. 21

Great Britain

In re Pinochet (House of Lords, January 15, 1999), ch. 2, fns. 34, 35

Canada

D. L. D., 77 CCC 3d 426, ch. 1, fn. 8
R. v. Lavallee, S.C.R. 852 (1990), ch. 8, fn. 6
Regina v. Grandjambe, 108 CCC 3d 338 (1996), ch. 4, fn. 33
WKL v. R., 64 CCC 3d 321, ch. 1, fn. 9

New Zealand

H. v. R., 1 NZLR 299 (1996), ch. 4, fn. 49

South Africa

Azanian Peoples Organization, Biko, and others v. the President of the Republic of South Africa and others, 1996 Case CCT 17/96 (CC), ch. 1, fns. 15, 19

United States Cases

Burdick v. United States, 236 U.S. 79 (1915), ch. 5, fn. 4
California v. Franklin, rev'd Franklin v. Duncan, 884 F.Supp. 1435 (N.D. Cal. 1995), ch. 1, fn. 23; ch. 7, fn. 3
Crider v. State, 531 N.E.2d 1151 (Ind. 1989), ch. 4, fn. 26
Danielski v. State, 48 N.W.2d 352 (Minn. 1984), ch. 4, fn. 28
De Rose v. Cardwell, 242 Cal. Reptr. 368 (1987), ch. 4, fn. 46
Demjanjuk v. United States, 10 F.3d 338 (6th Cir. 1993), ch. 1, fn. 25; ch. 6, fn. 67
Dusky v. United States, 362 U.S. 402 (1960), ch. 4, fn. 30
E. W. v. D. C. H., 754 P.2d 817 (Mont. 1988), ch. 4, fn. 47
Garland, 71 U.S. (4 Wall.) 333, 380 (1867), ch. 5, fn. 3
Hammer v. Hammer, 418 N.W.2d 23 (Wisc. 1987), ch. 4, fn. 48
Order of R. R. Telegraphers v. Railway Express Agency, 321 U.S. 342, 348 (1944), ch. 4, fn. 35
Schick v. Reed, 419 U.S. 256, 273 n8 (1974), ch. 5, fn. 5
State v. Bently, 721 P.2d 227 (Kan. 1986), ch. 4, fn. 25

AUTHOR INDEX

Numbers in italics refer to listings in endnotes.

SUBJECT INDEX

Numbers in italics refer to listings in endnotes.

ABOUT THE AUTHORS

Daniel Shuman is a professor of law at Southern Methodist University School of Law in Dallas, TX. He received his JD in 1972 from the University of Arizona. His other works include *Psychiatric and Psychological Evidence* (winner of the American Psychiatric Association's Manfred S. Guttmacher Award 1988), *Conducting Insanity Defense Evaluations* (with R. Rogers), *The Psychotherapist–Patient Privilege: A Critical Examination* (with M. Weiner), *Law and Mental Health Professionals: Texas* (American Psychological Association), *Doing Legal Research: A Guide for Social Scientists and Mental Health Professionals* (with R. Morris and B. Sales), and *Law, Mental Health, and Mental Disorder* (coeditor with B. Sales). He has also authored more than 60 articles and book chapters. His main areas of interest are in the field of law and mental health.

Alexander McCall Smith is a professor of law at the University of Edinburgh, Edinburgh, Scotland. He received his LLB and PhD from the University of Edinburgh. He has been a visiting professor at Southern Methodist University School of Law in Dallas, TX, as well as at universities in Africa and Italy. He is the author of numerous books in the area of criminal and medical law, including *Law and Medical Ethics* (with J. K. Mason), *Butterworths Medico-Legal Encyclopaedia* (with E. Sutherland), *Scots Criminal Law* (with D. Sheldon), *The Criminal Law of Botswana* (with K. Frimpong), *Introduzione allo Diritto Penale Scozzese* [Introduction to the Study of Scottish Criminal Law] (with A. Cadoppi), and the editor of several books, including *The Duty to Rescue* (with M. Menlowe) and *Forensic Aspects of Sleep* (with C. Shapiro). His main areas of interest are in medical law and criminal law.